Kristel Baldoz
Pushes Boundaries
Through Multidisciplinary Art

Buket Erdogan
Britain's Greatness Lies In Its Blend

MOSAIC DIGEST

Issue 5
JAN 2026
mosaicdigest.com

Boundless Brilliance

Stories That

Inspire

MARY ALICE MOLGARD

JANNA YESHANOVA

HALE EKINCI

PERRY OFFER

WOWART

A Journey Through Creative Minds

Available in print, electronic and online.
https://wowwart.com

A good book will keep you fascinated for days. A good bookshop for your whole life.

Waterstones

FICTION FAVORITES

Curated Novels to Enrich Your Reading Journey

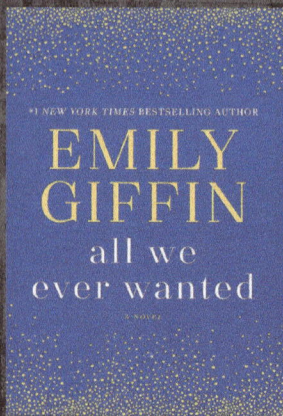

All We Ever Wanted
EMILY GIFFIN

"Page-turning . . . Timely and thought-provoking, it's Giffin's best yet."
—People

https://amzn.to/3WNATEc

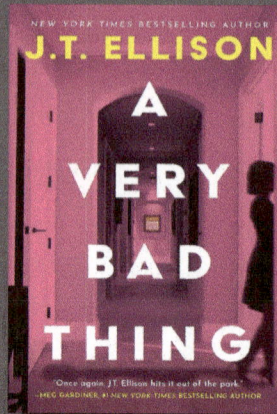

A Very Bad Thing
J.T. ELLISON

"A Very Bad Thing is a wonderfully smart, twisty psychological thriller infused with dark secrets, high drama, and edgy tension. Wow, what a ride!"
—Jayne Ann Krentz, New York Times bestselling author

https://amzn.to/4c41ktK

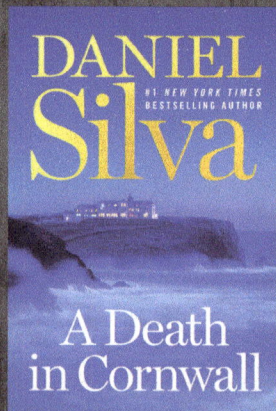

A Death in Cornwall
DANIEL SILVA

"Vastly entertaining with a blend of familiar characters, unrivaled plot development acumen, and artful repartee"
— J McIver

https://amzn.to/3WPoOyx

The Lions of Fifth Avenue
FIONA DAVIS

"The Lions of Fifth Avenue is a book written for booklovers."
—O, The Oprah Magazine

https://amzn.to/3LPu7al

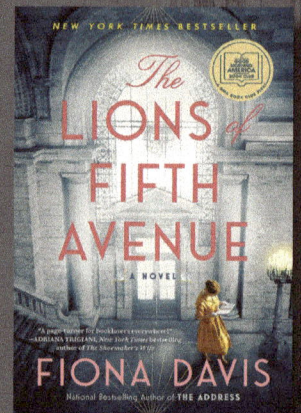

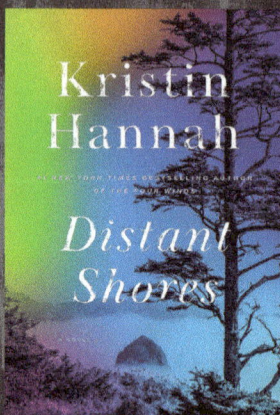

Distant Shores
KRISTIN HANNAH

"Certain to strike a chord . . . winning characterizations . . . and a few surprises."
—The Seattle Times

https://amzn.to/4d8uuco

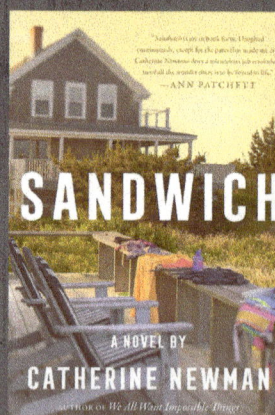

Sandwich
CATHERINE NEWMAN

"If you want a book that has you from 'hello,' this is the one."
— Ann Patchett, PBS NewsHour

https://amzn.to/3yb2shu

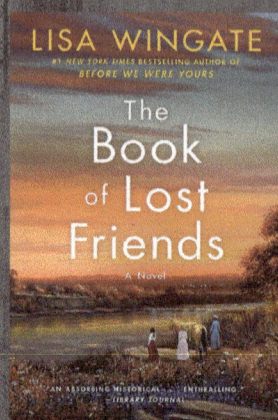

The Book of Lost Friends
LISA WINGATE

"A [story] of a family lost and found . . . a poignant, engrossing tale about sibling love and the toll of secrets."
— People

https://amzn.to/3WmZloY

Clete
JAMES LEE BURKE

"James Lee Burke is the reigning champ of nostalgia noir."
—New York Times Book Review

https://amzn.to/3LMAlmv

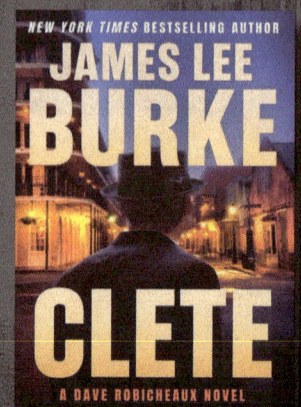

FICTION FAVORITES

Curated Novels to Enrich Your Reading Journey

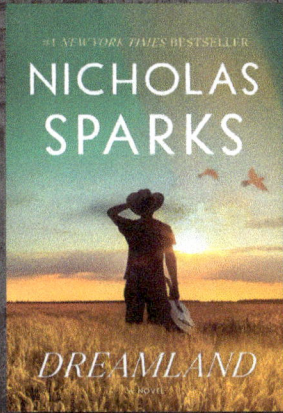

Dreamland
NICHOLAS SPARKS

"From this singular work it's clear that [Sparks] . . . continues to hone his craft."
—The Cullman Times

https://amzn.to/3Yx5tTR

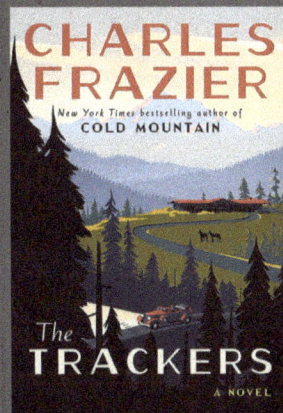

The Trackers
CHARLES FRAZIER

"Frazier is in top form.... Period-authentic, and the writing hums with spectacular word-images.... [A] propulsive tale of individualistic characters striving to beat the odds."
— Booklist (starred review)

https://amzn.to/3WwTWRJ

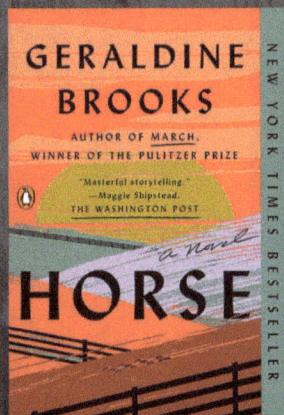

Horse
GERALDINE BROOKS

"[A] deft novel . . . create[s] a picture of the artistic, athletic, and scientific passions that horses can inspire in humans."
—The New Yorker

https://amzn.to/4d6exne

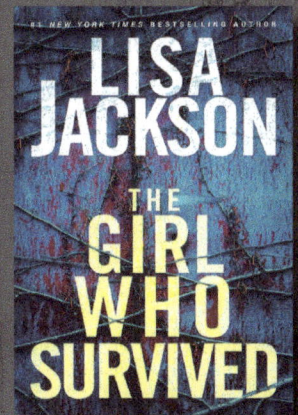

The Girl Who Survived
LISA JACKSON

This suspenseful thriller is packed with jaw-dropping twists."
—InTouch

https://amzn.to/3A0VUlR

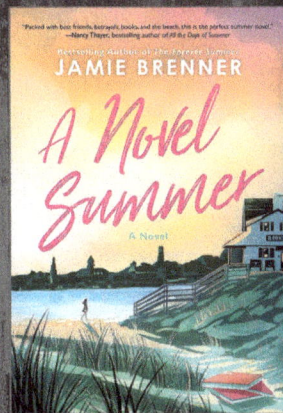

A Novel Summer
JAMIE BRENNER

"The perfect summer beach read! Rival bookshops, second chance romance, friend drama, it was the perfect book to curl up and escape to the Cape."
—Pamela Kelley, bestselling author of Bookshop by the Bay

https://amzn.to/3WtdCpF

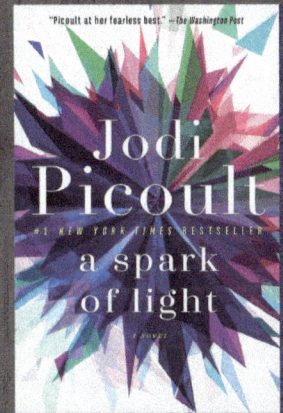

A Spark of Light
JODI PICOULT

"Picoult at her fearless best . . . Timely, balanced and certain to inspire debate."
—The Washington Post

https://amzn.to/3SzeesG

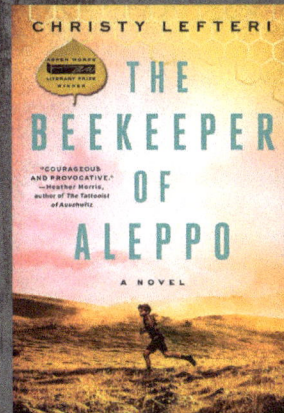

The Beekeeper of Aleppo
CHRISTY LEFTERI

"Beekeeper Nuri and his wife, Afra, are devastated by the Syrian civil war. After violence claims their child and Afra's eyesight, the couple is forced to flee Aleppo and make the fraught journey to Britain—and an uncertain future."
—USA Today

https://amzn.to/4dsnhnu

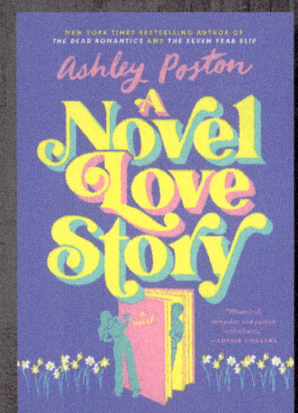

A Novel Love Story
ASHLEY POSTON

"Ashley Poston has written another clever, emotional love story part fantasy, part romcom—perfect for passing a day or three by the pool."
—Harper's Bazaar

https://amzn.to/3WKwcLt

What's INSIDE

Words & Worlds: A Journey Through Expert Perspectives

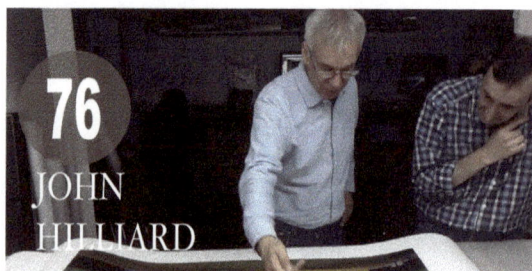

PUBLISHER: Mosaic Digest, A Subsidiary of NewYox Media Group. 200 Suite 134-146 Curtain Road, EC2A 3AR London, United Kingdom
t: +44 79 3847 8420 editor@mosaicdigest.com II http://newyox.com
EDITORIAL: Hazel Ivy, Editor-in-Chief, Arch Preston, Managing Editor, C. Rochelle, Art Editor, Delfina Reneta, Content Editor,
Reporters: Jack Wilson, Jenny Taylor , J. Evans, Amy Browm CONTRIBUTOS: Claudine D. Reyes, Esma Arslan, Adrian T.
We assume no responsibility for unsolicited manuscripts or art materials provided from our contributors.

EDITOR'S LETTER

Welcome to the latest edition of *Mosaic Digest*, where every story sparks inspiration, and every angle brings us closer to understanding the extraordinary. This issue is a celebration of the human spirit—of passion, perseverance, and the courage to transform dreams into reality. Through these pages, you'll meet innovators, creators, and trailblazers from diverse walks of life, each leaving their mark in unique ways.

Our featured interviews spotlight individuals from myriad fields—artists, authors, educators, entrepreneurs, and visionaries—who have pushed boundaries and redefined success. From classrooms to stages, from high seas to corporate boardrooms, their journeys transcend challenges, reminding us of the resilience and creativity that bind us all.

Among the voices we bring you is Mary Alice Molgard, a legendary communicator and educator who has not only built an enduring legacy in radio, television, and public affairs but also mentored countless students, including the likes of Jimmy Fallon. Her reflections on her dynamic career and her advice on staying adaptable feel like a masterclass in persistence and reinvention.

We explore bold horizons with Alexis Anicque, whose storytelling blends real-life adventure with fantasy, offering both inspiration and escape. Living aboard a sailboat, she has transformed her travels into vivid narratives that encourage us all to embrace fearlessness in pursuit of our dreams.

Business innovator Perry Offer shares his compelling philosophy of simplicity—reminding us that cutting through complexity to focus on what truly matters is not just a business strategy but a mindset for modern life. His journey is a testament to the power of determination and clarity during times of uncertainty.

These compelling stories are just the beginning. From artists capturing humanity in every brushstroke to entrepreneurs rewriting the rules of success, and authors whose words transport us to other worlds, this issue is an ode to those who dare to be different.

At *Mosaic Digest,* we believe that stories have the power to connect, inspire, and transform. Each feature in this edition reflects that belief, offering readers the chance to see the world through the eyes of people driven by passion, vision, and ingenuity. Their stories remind us to embrace our creativity, celebrate our individuality, and remain steadfast in the pursuit of our own unique paths.

Thank you for joining us on this journey through inspiration and insight. May these voices spark your imagination, ignite your ambition, and remind you of the beauty in chasing big dreams.

Warmly,

Hazel

Editor-in-Chief

What's IN

Perry Offer discusses his philosophy of simplicity in business, outlining how it transformed Wood Hosiery into a market leader while fostering resilience and adaptability to overcome modern challenges in the corporate environment.

PUBLISHER: Mosaic Digest, A Subsidiary of NewYox Media Group. 200 Suite 134-146 Curtain Road, EC2A 3AR London, United Kingdom
t: +44 79 3847 8420 editor@mosaicdigest.com ‖ http://newyox.com
EDITORIAL: Hazel Ivy, Editor-in-Chief, Arch Preston, Managing Editor, C. Rochelle, Art Editor, Delfina Reneta, Content Editor,
Reporters: Jack Wilson, Jenny Taylor , J. Evans, Amy Browm CONTRIBUTOS: Claudine D. Reyes, Esma Arslan, Adrian T.
We assume no responsibility for unsolicited manuscripts or art materials provided from our contributors.

SIDE

Buket Erdoğan: A Leading Voice in Immigration Law and Advocacy, Combining Expertise With a Passion for Innovation and Fairness

From the Classroom to the American Red Cross

MARY ALICE MOLGARD

Reflects on Four Decades of Transforming the Communications World

BY ELEANOR WILSON

Mary Alice Molgard is a name synonymous with passion, resilience, and innovation in the evolving world of communications. A beacon of excellence throughout her remarkable 40-year career in radio, television, film, and education, Mary Alice has carved an enduring legacy as both a practitioner and a mentor. She is not just a storyteller but a devoted architect of futures, having launched countless careers and inspired generations of students during her 36 years of teaching at the College of Saint Rose. Today, her unwavering commitment to service continues through her impactful work in Public Affairs for the American Red Cross of Northeastern New York, where she transforms words into action and compassion into results.

At *Mosaic Digest* magazine, we celebrate extraordinary individuals who shape our world through their talent and integrity, and Mary Alice Molgard is undeniably one of those figures. Her journey from a young college student captivated by a college radio station to becoming a force in communications education and disaster response is nothing short of remarkable. Whether she's recounting her experiences guiding students

like Jimmy Fallon to stardom, sharing her expertise on adapting to an ever-changing field, or reflecting on the joy of seeing her graduates thrive in diverse pursuits, Mary Alice embodies the power of persistence and a lifelong commitment to learning.

In this exclusive interview, we had the privilege of sitting down with Mary Alice Molgard to delve into her decades of experience,

Mary Alice Molgard shares her incredible journey from radio beginnings to shaping countless careers as an educator, while navigating the ever-changing communications field with passion and adaptability.

her thoughts on the evolution of communications, and her insights on cultivating success in today's dynamic world. It is an honor to feature the wisdom and achievements of someone who has left an indelible mark not only on her students and colleagues but on an entire industry. This conversation is a testament to the transformative power of education, the importance of adaptability, and the enduring impact of one individual's dedication to her craft and community.

What originally inspired you to pursue a career in radio, television, film, and communications?

Originally, I intended to pursue print journalism, but as a high school senior I lost the chance at a scholarship to a prestigious j-school and became disenchanted. I

enrolled as an Archaeology and Anthropology major, but that didn't last long. I was introduced to new friends who worked at the college radio station. They invited me to take a tour, and I was hooked. I changed my major to Communications and fell in love with radio and television. I worked with a wonderful group of professors who had both academic and real-life broadcast experience. Under their guidance, I became passionate about news and communications law, and the rest is history! I spent the next 40+ years working in Communications, as an educator and practitioner.

Can you share any standout moments or highlights from your 36 years of teaching at the College of Saint Rose?

I literally helped create the program I taught in for 36 years. When I began my career at the College, the major had been officially established but there were only a handful of real Communications courses. The others were borrowed from other majors. A colleague and I planned a curriculum and then created the courses to fill it over a two-year period. The major grew rapidly, and soon Communications was one of the largest on campus. That was probably the greatest moment, but I considered graduation each year to be its own highlight. I had the pleasure of seeing students I had taught, persuaded, mothered, and maybe even gently threatened walk across the stage. I was thrilled they had persevered. Some were A students; others were not. I think I was more thrilled with the C students' success because most of them

Mary Alice Molgard: A distinguished mentor, communications pioneer, and dedicated advocate for humanitarian efforts with the American Red Cross.

worked harder than their peers to get their degrees.

How has the field of communications evolved over the course of your career, and how did you adapt your teaching to reflect those changes?

I'm old school. I always believed if you could write for radio, you could write for any medium.

I would paint a picture for the listener with words and sound, editing audio tape with a razor blade, but when the industry focus shifted more to television, I had a hard time adapting. I had to learn new rules, procedures, and technologies all at the same time. It was a challenge! But I did it by centering on true content creation, the scripts, the news stories, the ad copy. I became a producer rather than a technician. I'm pretty good at telling a video editor where I want the clip to begin or end, and where to drop in the audio. Then I encourage them do their magic with the computer and keyboard. Some people are wired for that process. I'm not one of them. I believe that you can craft and deliver a creative and effective story, no matter the medium.

How do you think young professionals can best prepare for success in the ever-changing field of communications today?

It's very simple. Never stop learning about your chosen field, even if you are already employed in it. Read every quality, legitimate media source you can get your hands on. Newspapers, blogs, magazines. Watch national news and local news. This may not be the most popular current opinion, but don't fall for the nonsense that the mainstream media somehow has become evil. Use social media to your advantage but avoid the garbage that seems to ooze from it. You need to know about the world outside your immediate frame of reference. That means having at least basic familiarity with geography, international relations, economics, and how governmental systems operate. Not only do you need to know how to communicate, but you also need to have enough information to communicate about something.

Internships are the best way to get pre-employment experience, but volunteering for not-for-profit organizations is helpful too. You get to work on every aspect of the organization and can make contacts that are invaluable for the future. If employed in the field, the young professional needs to find a balance between completing day-to-day responsibilities and reaching for new experiences. Learning the requirements

Mary Alice Molgard reflects on her significant influence in shaping the careers of many young talents, noting how the path to stardom for comedian Jimmy Fallon intersected with hers during his time at the College of Saint Rose. Image Credit: HiClipArt

THE TONIGHT SHOW STARRING JIMMY FALLON

and limitations of a new job is important and can't be ignored, but the YP also needs to be aware of how to position themselves to take advantage of new opportunities.

During your time teaching, you had many talented students. Can you share any memorable stories about them, Jimmy Fallon for instance, during his time as your student?

Jimmy was nearing the end of his senior year and came to me for some advice. I was the internship coordinator and helped all the seniors find internships. He had been offered the chance to go off to do stand-up comedy, but it meant he would have to leave school. He had only one semester to finish his degree, and I advised him not to throw it all away. He ignored my advice, thankfully, and launched himself into what has become an amazing career. A few years ago, I went to the Tonight Show to see him, and during a break in the show, he came up into the audience and had me tell all 400 people about the worst mistake in judgement in my professional life!

What was it like watching one of your students, like Jimmy Fallon, rise to such incredible fame? How did it make you feel? Can you name any other former students who went on to accomplish impressive things in their careers?

While Jimmy Fallon is probably the most recognizable of my former students, there are many who have been remarkably successful. I am thrilled with all their successes. Social media has made it possible for me to follow their careers, and I'm just as thrilled with the young woman who launched an incredibly successful local cookie company as with the CEO of a major charitable foundation. Among the most notable are a National Public Radio reporter, a producer at MSNBC, another at CBS, a reality show actress who recently launched a clothing line, a New York State trooper, even the publisher of an international magazine...Shall I go on? I've literally got hundreds of them.

Did you ever suspect that Jimmy Fallon or any of your other students would achieve the kind of success they did while they were studying at the College of Saint Rose?

Every semester when I would look out over a crop of new students, I would be ho-

peful that each would realize their potential. For some, the goal was simply getting a degree and a job. Others would prove to be more ambitious and reach for something that was a little more out there on the horizon. What I wanted for them was to develop the knowledge and skills they would need to be successful no matter what they chose to pursue. In a class of 50 students, maybe one achieves some level of notoriety. If the other 49 found something they were good at and were satisfied or even happy, I'd be just as thrilled. Their success is my reward.

Now that you're working in Public Affairs for the American Red Cross of Northeastern New York, what are some of the projects or initiatives you're most passionate about?

Are there any specific challenges or rewarding experiences you've encountered in your current role at the American Red Cross?

The mission of the American Red Cross is to prevent and alleviate human suffering. My small part in the mission is to create messaging that advances that goal and do my best to engage local media with our activities. I work closely with local reporters when there is a large-scale national incident, helping arrange interviews with volunteers who are deploying or are already on the ground in the disaster zone. I've reported on wildfires, hurricanes, floods, ice storms, just about every natural disaster you can think of. At the local level, helping get the word out about home fires is just as important as covering a hurricane. Press releases from my department detail the incident and describe the scope of assistance Red Cross provides. We supply financial assistance, help arrange for health services, and provide comfort and emotional support. I'm focused on making sure the public is aware of how easy it is to get the assistance they need. A current passion project is scanning blogs, websites, and social media pages to find mentions of home fires in our coverage area in order to connect displaced residents with Red Cross services.

Eileen Hobbs Brings Magic, Diversity And Realism To Children's Literature

BY MOSAIC DIGEST STAFF

Photo: *Eileen Hobbs, award-winning author of the Heath Cousins series, inspires young readers with her imaginative tales rooted in diversity and heartfelt themes.*

Exploring Fantasy Adventures And Real-Life Themes In Award-Winning Books

Eileen Hobbs masterfully creates enchanting worlds, empowering characters, and culturally rich narratives that inspire young readers to imagine and empathize.

Eileen Hobbs is a beacon of talent in the landscape of children's literature, combining imagination, emotion, and diverse representation in her award-winning works. The acclaimed author of the Heath Cousins series and stand-alone titles like *Under the Golden Rain Tree and Stella and the Sea Stars*, Hobbs transports her readers to magical realms while simultaneously tackling real-world issues such as cultural identity, resilience, and bullying. Her skillful storytelling bridges the fantastical with the relatable, making her books a treasure trove for young readers seeking adventure, understanding, and wonder.

A lifelong traveler and learner, Hobbs' multicultural upbringing in Thailand and her experiences as an English composition teacher for international students infuse her narratives with authenticity and depth. From vividly imagined adventures in magical gateways to heartfelt narratives grounded in real family dynamics, Hobbs crafts stories that resonate deeply with her audience. Her commitment to celebrating diversity and creating relatable, courageous characters shines through in every book, inspiring readers to explore the world—from the bustling streets of London to the serene beaches of Coral Island—with empathy and curiosity.

At Mosaic Digest magazine, we are thrilled to feature Eileen Hobbs as part of our dedication to exploring the brilliant minds behind today's most compelling literature. Through her riveting series, imaginative fantasy tales, and authentic cultural portrayals, Hobbs has earned accolades such as the Firebird Book Awards and Literary Titan recognitions, cementing her place as a powerful voice in children's storytelling. It is an honor to sit down with her and delve into the creative process that has enchanted countless readers and budding writers alike. Join us in celebrating a remarkable author whose vision continues to inspire and uplift, one story at a time.

You grew up in Thailand as the daughter of missionaries before settling in Oklahoma—how has that multicultural upbringing influenced your storytelling and the settings in your books?

It has influenced me in so many ways. Of course, Under the Golden Rain Tree is a direct result of growing up in Thailand and I always wanted to tell a story based in Thailand and include a lot of my own experiences in it.

For example, Thai games; eating fruit, like guava, bananas and mangoes; the influence of Buddhism; rice farming; buffaloes etc. I grew up with all of that! I grew up speaking Thai and I want kids to know how cool it is to learn a different language. That's why Addie B. can read and understand different languages with the Moonstone ring, because that's something I always wanted to do. But I also grew up traveling a lot in general and since many kids can't travel, I wanted to include different places and cultures in my books. The Ruby Lantern, for example, is inspired by my Asian upbringing and introduces Mai Li, from China. While I had the privilege of growing up in another country, many kids don't have that chance and I want kids to know that you can learn about other people and cultures by reading!

Your Heath Cousins series draws inspiration from the childhood games of your own children and their cousins—could you walk us through how those imaginative play sessions evolved into full-fledged fantasy adventures?

Eileen Hobbs masterfully creates enchanting worlds, empowering characters, and culturally rich narratives that inspire young readers to imagine and empathize.

I used to watch my two boys and their two cousins playing outside and using their imaginations. They would pretend to be kings and queens, sword fighting with tree limbs, running or chasing the enemy and other escapades. When I first saw this, I thought: wouldn't it be a great story about cousins that enter a magical land and have adventures? So that's when I started writing The Heath Cousins and the Moonstone Cave.

The Heath Cousins books span five titles, each with its own magical gateway—how do you ensure continuity and freshness across the series?

I did a lot of rereading of the previous book and tried to make sure that I was consistent from book to book. It was important to me that each character had challenges and growth from book to book while still maintaining their basic personalities. The "freshness" I think came from having the gateways in different locales – London, North Carolina, Maine – so I could include situations that fit in with that locale: British Museum in London, mountains in NC, caves in Maine etc.

Your stand-alone novels, such as Under the Golden Rain Tree and Stella and the Sea Stars, weave in real-world issues like bullying and family change—how do you strike the balance between addressing serious themes and maintaining a sense of wonder for young readers?

I don't know that I always have that balance but I hope so. There will always be

kids that can't relate to those themes but I just feel it's important to introduce difficult topics for kids because many of them are going through it already. However, I try not to dwell on it too heavily, and I try to intermix adventure and humor with it. I also try to show that you can face a lot of hard things with the help of good friends and your family. I also try to have an ending that may not solve everything but hopefully ends on a positive note.

Stella and the Sea Stars introduces readers to magic in a seaside setting while exploring divorce and resilience—what inspired this particular story, and how did place—such as Coral Island—shape the narrative?

First, I love the beach so much. My husband and I have a condo on the beach in Long Boat Key, Florida. Being there inspired Stella and the Sea Stars. I just loved the idea of Stella, who is going through a hard time due to her parents' divorce, going (reluctantly) to the beach, discovers about her own heritage, and learns more about her parents, especially her mom. This brings her closer to her mom and grandmom. I love stories about going through a hard time and then becoming closer to family or friends through it. But I love fantasy too, so I wanted to bring that element in with the Sea Stars. Stella realizes she is not alone and that she has a rich connection to the sea.

Diversity is a key value in your writing, featuring characters from various cultural backgrounds—how do you research and develop these characters authentically, and what feedback have you received from young readers?

My family is very diverse. My oldest son was adopted from Paraguay and my youngest son is part Native American. I grew up in Thailand and my husband grew up in Hong Kong. A lot of developing characters authentically comes from watching my boys grow up and hearing about their experiences as well as my many great nieces and nephews. It is important to include this diversity in my books because of my kids but also we are a diverse society and hopefully some kids will be able to identify with my characters because of that. Most of the feedback I get is positive, but kids are all so different, and their taste in books is different and I totally respect that.

You teach English composition to international students, which seems like rich inspiration for a writer—how does your teaching work feed into your writing, and vice versa?

I am retired from teaching now but I loved my international students. They were my window to the world. They were so smart and courageous to come study in another country. I think just being around them, hearing them tell about their culture and country – I absorbed a lot of that and could include it in my writing.

You've amassed quite a few accolades—from Firebird Book Awards to Literary Titan recognitions for titles like Ruby Lantern, Crystal Canyon, and

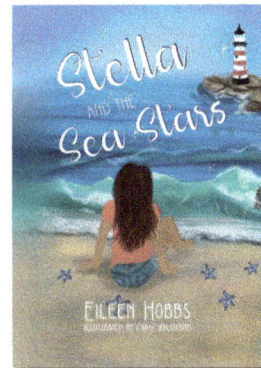

Silver Statue—what have been the most meaningful award moments for you, and how have they impacted your career?

They have all been wonderful award moments but I guess my first award, for Crystal Canyon, stands out. It was at the Bookfest Awards Ceremony and I was called up on stage and recognized. I was so happy that night and felt so honored. I'm not sure if the awards have impacted my career per se, but each one gives me confidence to keep going and to keep writing. I suffer with the imposter syndrome still.

Having visited schools and engaged young readers in creative activities—from read-alouds to crafting gemstone necklaces—what do these interactions teach you about your audience, and how do they influence your future stories?

I love talking to kids about their interests. They are just so smart and funny. I love teaching them Thai words to share with their parents! I find out what they are reading, what they like about the stories. They give me such great ideas. "You should write about a worm hole, or do a sequel to The Heath Cousins, or write about zombies." So far, only the sequel is in the works. They also share their stories with me – what they have written – and that makes me so happy too. They are my inspiration for sure!

Lastly, for fellow or emerging children's authors, what advice would you offer—whether about crafting fantasy grounded in real emotion, balancing diverse representation, or maintaining authenticity while addressing challenging topics?

Write about what you love because that will definitely come through in your writing. If you love zombies, write about zombies! If you love Pikachu, write about an adventure you had with Pikachu. Don't worry so much about the grammar, style etc. especially in your first draft. Just let the story take you away. Keep a notebook of your stories. I

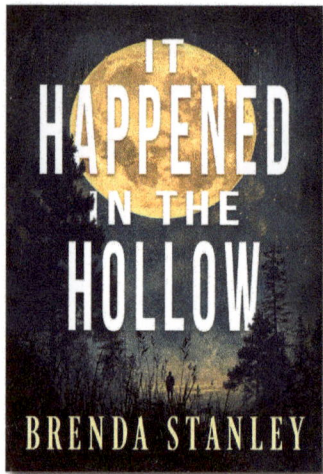

Brenda Stanley Inspires Readers Through Suspense, Secrets, And Emotional Connections

Author Brenda Stanley shares her creative journey, blending suspense, emotional depth, and personal experiences to craft gripping novels and explore themes of family, secrets, and resilience with authenticity.

By Carine O'Leary

Brenda Stanley masterfully intertwines suspense and emotional depth in *It Happened in the Hollow*. This hauntingly beautiful novel explores grief, guilt, and the power of human connection as Landis and Benji navigate the secrets hidden within the Idaho woods. Stanley's vivid descriptions bring the setting to life, while the dual perspectives of the living and the dead add an intriguing layer of complexity. With compelling characters and a gripping mystery, this story is both poignant and thrilling, leaving readers captivated until the very last page. A must-read for fans of soulful suspense.

Brenda Stanley is, without question, a literary force to be reckoned with—a writer whose extraordinary talent defies boundaries and genres. With suspenseful plots that keep readers on edge and emotionally complex characters that leave lasting impressions, her novels are the kind of stories you carry with you long after the final page. Drawing inspiration from her dynamic life experiences—whether as a tenacious investigative journalist, an Idaho ranch owner, or a mother navigating the intricacies of a large family—Brenda seamlessly blends authenticity, depth, and intrigue into every book she writes.

Brenda Stanley, an author whose works reveal the profound humanity nestled within the darkest secrets and the resilience found in even the most fragile connections. As Brenda shares the fascinating journey behind her craft, including the inspiration for her upcoming novel *It Happened in the Hollow*, readers will gain insight into the boundless curiosity and heartfelt passion that make her stories resonate so deeply. Brenda Stanley is not just a storyteller; she's an architect of emotion, and her ability to weave together mystery, history, and human connection is nothing short of remarkable. This interview is not to be missed.

What inspired you to start writing novels, and how did you develop your style of incorporating suspense and mystery?

I have always loved to read and that inspired my desire to write. My father worked in law enforcement and as an undercover agent for the DEA. This shaped my writing style by instilling a strong sense of suspense, attention to detail, and a fascination with the hidden motives behind people's actions.

How has your background as a television news anchor and investigative reporter influenced your approach to storytelling?

My career as an investigative journalist taught me how to dig beneath the surface, ask the right questions, and tell compelling, fact-driven stories. That experience shaped my fiction by giving me a strong sense of pacing, character motivation, and how to weave suspense through real-world details that make a story feel authentic and urgent.

Can you share your experience of writing your first novel at the age of seventeen and how it shaped your journey as an author?

When I wrote my first novel, I was a teen mom. I was living in a very rural and isolated part of Utah, and reading and writing were what I did to escape the loneliness and uncertainty of that time. Writing became my refuge—a way to process everything I was going through and to imagine a world beyond my immediate reality.

What elements of life in Idaho and your small ranch inspire your settings and characters?

Many of my stories evolve from what I see and experience here in Idaho and on my own property. I love to ride horses in the mountains and hike in the woods. My stories often feature these elements. My most recent novel even incorporates fly fishing into the storyline.

How do you balance creating intriguing suspenseful plots with the emotional depth of your characters?

For me, the key to balancing suspense with emotional depth is making sure the plot serves the characters, not the other way around. I start with people—flawed, complex, and real—and let their fears, secrets, and desires drive the tension. Suspense isn't just about what's happening; it's about why it matters to the characters, when readers care about who's at the center of the storm, every twist and reveal hits that much harder.

What was the creative process like for your upcoming book, "It Happened in the Hollow," and what inspired the story?

I wanted to tell this story from two perspectives—one grounded in the present, and one looking in from beyond the veil. That structure allowed me to weave together past and present, showing how long-buried truths still shape the lives unfolding now. I spent a considerable amount of time researching Idaho's history, particularly the rivers and waterways that serve as the state's lifeblood. It's not just fiction—people have truly been killed over land and water rights. Fly fishing became the perfect vehicle to connect two generations with the river.

How do your personal experiences, such as being a mother of five and your connection to family, influence the themes in your novels?

Being a mother of five has deeply shaped the way I write about relationships, resilience, and the bonds that hold us together, even when they're messy or strained. Family, in all its complexity, is at the heart of my stories. I'm especially drawn to the impact of family secrets—how what's hidden or unspoken can echo through generations. My personal experience helps me write characters who love fiercely, fight hard, and carry both joy and pain with them, just like real families do, especially when the past refuses to stay buried.

What challenges do you face in maintaining uniqueness and creativity in your various novels?

One of the biggest challenges is ensuring that each story feels fresh while remaining true to my voice. I never want to repeat a plot or character arc just because it worked before. To keep things unique, I dig deeper into new themes, settings, or emotional truths I haven't explored yet. It also helps to stay curious about people, history, and even my own fears. Creativity comes from simply asking, What if?

How do you approach weaving intricate and mysterious storylines without giving away too much too soon?

I approach it like a puzzle—revealing just enough pieces at a time to keep readers curious, but not so much that they can see the whole picture too early. I also write my endings first, so I know where my story is leading, and it helps me keep the complex twists from deviating from where I need them to go. It's all about timing and perspective. I use character emotions, setting, and subtle clues to build tension, trusting the reader to pick up on what's between the lines. Holding back just the right details creates that sense of unease and anticipation that makes a mystery compelling.

What advice would you give to aspiring authors who want to write compelling and emotionally resonant stories?

Write the story that scares you a little—the one that feels personal, vulnerable, or deeply honest. That's where the emotional resonance lives. Don't be afraid to dig into your own experiences and truths, because authenticity is what makes a story stick with readers. Also, spend time getting to know your characters; the more real they feel to you, the more real they'll feel to others.

Brenda Stanley: Masterfully weaving mystery, history, and emotion, the acclaimed author captivates readers with unforgettable characters and gripping, suspenseful narratives.

Suspense isn't just about what's happening; it's about why it matters to the characters."

Brenda Stanley

Exploring Love, Laughter, And Lifelong Creativity

Donna McDonald Shares How Humor, Strong Heroines And Resilience Shape Her Remarkable Multi-Genre Writing Journey

Donna McDonald, USA Today Bestselling Author, discusses her multi-genre writing journey, creative process, resilience after personal loss, and her commitment to crafting strong heroines and relatable, joyful romances.

By Carine O'Leary

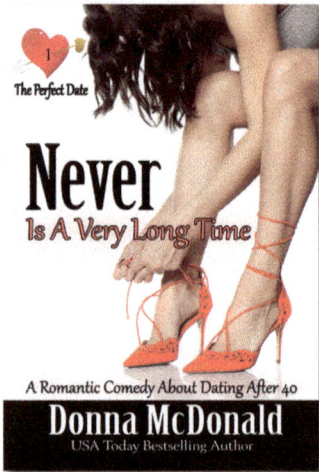

Donna McDonald's *Never Is A Very Long Time* is a delightful romantic comedy packed with humor, heart, and relatable characters. Dr. Mariah Bates navigates love, heartbreak, and reinvention with charm and resilience, making readers cheer for her every step of the way. With witty banter, laugh-out-loud moments, and a sprinkle of rekindled hope, this vibrant story celebrates finding love later in life. Perfect for readers craving romance with real-life challenges and plenty of laughs!

Donna McDonald is the quintessential storyteller who reminds us all that it's never too late to answer the call of creativity. With over a decade of publishing success and nearly one hundred books to her name, she has captivated readers across a spectrum of genres—from swoon-worthy contemporary romances to adrenaline-packed science fiction and paranormal tales. Donna's signature blend of humor, heart, and relatable heroines has solidified her place not only as a USA Today Bestselling Author but as a beloved voice that dares to challenge genre conventions and societal norms.

Dubbed the queen of mature romance, Donna brings life to characters who often go overlooked in traditional narratives—proving that love, adventure, and personal growth don't come with an expiration date. Whether she's crafting heartbreakingly human cyborg soldiers, tenacious action heroines, or independent, witty women navigating love later in life, Donna's ability to infuse both depth and levity into her stories is unmatched. Through her heartwarming and hilarious tales, she's taught her readers not just to believe in second chances, but to revel in them.

In this exclusive interview, we delve into the life and mind behind the stories. Donna opens up about how a personal tragedy became the spark for her writing career, the importance of laughter in fiction, and her philosophy on creating complex worlds and even more complex characters. Get ready to be inspired by an author who doesn't just write happy endings—she builds them, one story at a time.

What inspired you to start writing romance novels after a long career in other fields?

I'm a voracious reader and have always been a writer of some sort. Regardless of how I made money, publishing a book remained on my "to-do-one-day" list. I wish I could say I made it happen by simply sitting down to write, but that wasn't the case. In 2009, my oldest daughter was diagnosed with stage four cancer. I took care of her during the last year of her life and didn't recover quickly from her loss. A few months after she died, I started writing. Weeks later, I discovered I had written 75,000 words. It was a bittersweet triumph to finally type "The End" and know it was a complete, finished story. You could say writing rescued me from my grief, and you wouldn't be wrong. I prefer writing fiction with happily-ever-after or happy-for-now endings because real life does not offer those to everyone. I enjoy having

the power to create them in my fiction.

How do you balance humor with romance in your stories to keep readers engaged?

Love and romance are essential elements in most successful stories. Humor can provide a chance to breathe during tense conflicts. Also, laughter heals. A character with a quirky sense of humor is fun, and rooting for them is natural and easy. My readers love my stories because they know I will leave them smiling, no matter what happens in the plot. Bad things do happen in my fiction, but the good guys always win—always. If someone wants stark reality, the news can provide that. I prefer to grant wishes for my struggling characters and offer my readers a mental escape into a world where life works out.

Can you share how your "writer vacation" into science fiction and paranormal romance evolved into a full-fledged passion?

Initially, I aspired to write science fiction, paranormal, and fantasy stories. Female action and adventure characters were, and remain, relatively uncommon outside of Urban Fantasy and Paranormal Romance. You don't find many mature, kick-butt heroines in "mainstream" novels. When I first started publishing in 2011, I decided my contemporary romances with older characters would best set me apart in the indie author world. I defied the norms and wrote sexy, love-drenched, sensual romances with older characters. Back then, I would tell my contemporary readers that they would have to wait a bit for their next book because I was writing a science fiction story. I referred to it as my "writing vacation" because I thought they would understand that best. Variety is critical to my creativity.

What challenges do you face when creating believable romantic relationships involving complex sci-fi or paranormal elements?

World-building in science fiction and fantasy novels requires readers to suspend their normal beliefs to fully enjoy the story. My job is to make it worth a reader's time to believe that my scientifically created werewolves use nanotechnology to survive shifting, while they remain human enough to want to find love. When I wrote my cyborg series, the focus was on restoring each cyber soldier's humanity, with all that entails. I try to align my "science fiction" as closely with reality as possible for relatability. That is not possible with werewolves and dragons, so I don't bother to do that in fantasies.

How has your own life experience influenced your decision to write about older characters finding love?

Trite but true, it was me just writing about what I knew. I was fifty-two when I published my first novel. My first contemporary romance heroine was turning fifty and wondering if life had passed her by. She was a divorced businesswoman with an adult daughter. She ran a business, had assistants, and still made time for her friends. Why wouldn't I want to write about a woman that strong and unstoppable? Sex, romance, and love do not suddenly end at thirty-five. Never Too Late is not just my first series title. It's my mantra for living my life.

What has been the most rewarding feedback you've received from readers about your portrayal of mature romance?

This list is lengthy because I have the best readers in the world, but I will focus on the top few. Some readers wrote to say my older characters inspired them to date again after losing a spouse, giving up, or surviving a horrific illness. Some wrote to say they read my work while keeping vigil at the side of a hospitalized loved one, and I lightened their hearts with my humor. Others mentioned they enjoyed reading an author who always made them laugh. The money I earn from sales enables me to continue writing, but these messages from readers are the actual proof of my success.

How do you develop strong, relatable heroines who also fit into humorous romantic comedies?

My characters are relatable because I find most people fascinating. Long before I met my humor-writing friend, I wanted to learn to craft humor. I had no money for formal classes, so I pulled out my favorite "chick flick" romantic comedies and turned on the director's cut. Nora Ephron and Nancy Meyers became my teachers. They discussed "in this scene…" and explained their choices. I took notes on timing, character development, and flow. Afterward, I wrote scenes and then went back and added what I thought of as "the funny" parts.

Could you explain your creative process for world-building in your science fiction romance series?

One book is never enough to tell the entire story my mind imagines, especially when showing character development through a variety of character-building experiences. Series are just natural for me. When I begin a new series, little movies featuring the newly created main character run through my mind. If the characters are happy with themselves and me, the mind movies multiply and connect to others. Before I know it, I'm immersed in the new world and become obsessed with finding words for it.

What advice do you have for authors who want to write across multiple genres without losing their unique voice?

I have no advice. If they end up needing to write across genres, as I did, I can only wish them the best of luck. I'm living a happy, creative life as a multi-genre author, but from a business standpoint, there is no doubt that I traded profit for creativity. Following my muse sounds noble, and it occasionally feels courageous, but it won't pay the bills unless I work tirelessly to sell each genre to the proper audience.

What is the most important piece of advice you would give to aspiring romance authors starting their writing journey?

Write the books of your heart because those stories will naturally resonate with the right readers. I'm preparing to release my one hundredth book

. I know that writing this one will be just as enjoyable as writing the first. Writing is my life, and I aim to create books until the end of my days. I would advise them not to forget to celebrate each book because every book deserves its own moment to shine, just as its author does.

Writing rescued me from my grief, and you wouldn't be wrong.

Donna McDonald
USA TODAY BESTSELLING AUTHO

Donna McDonald: Celebrating Over A Decade Of Multi-Genre Mastery And Uplifting Stories That Bring Humor, Heart, And Hope To Readers Everywhere

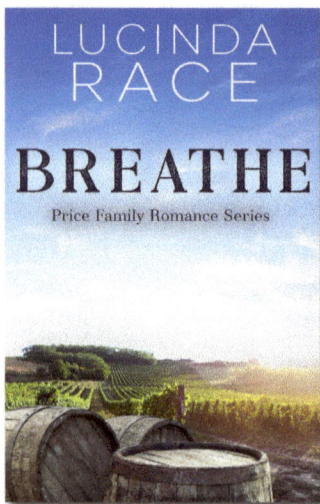

Lucinda Race Blends Cozy Mysteries and Romance with Heart, Hope and Paranormal Charm

Lucinda Race discusses her writing process, blending paranormal elements with cozy mysteries, creating relatable characters, and crafting emotionally rich stories inspired by her life and travels.

by Carine O'Leary

Lucinda Race's *Breathe* delivers a heartfelt small-town romance. Tessa Price's determination to revive the struggling Sand Creek Winery and prove her worth is both inspiring and compelling. The chemistry between Tessa and Max Maxwell, the former owner with a brooding charm, builds naturally, weaving tension and tenderness into their partnership. As secrets unearth and emotions deepen, the story balances romance, resilience, and family dynamics beautifully.

With its rich vineyard setting and emotional stakes, this first installment in the Price Family Romance Series offers a flavorful blend of passion and hope. Perfect for fans of small-town love!

Lucinda Race's literary world is a treasure trove of emotion, imagination, and endearing characters that draw readers into heartfelt romances and captivating mysteries. With a talent for crafting tales brimming with intrigue and joy, Lucinda has become a beacon of inspiration in the literary community. Her ability to create small-town settings that feel as familiar as home—yet packed with surprises around every corner—underscores her mastery of storytelling.

Through her beloved McKenna Family Romance series and her uniquely enchanting Paranormal Cozy Nook Bookstore series, Lucinda skillfully fuses the sweetness of clean romance with the thrill of suspenseful murder plots. The charm of her writing lies in her versatility—whether it's a talking familiar in a cozy mystery or the emotional depth of finding love later in life, Lucinda's stories appeal to readers of all ages and genres.

As you read this exclusive Novelist Post interview, you'll glimpse the creative brilliance and personal warmth that make Lucinda Race not only a celebrated author but also a cherished voice in contemporary fiction. From inspiration drawn from her adorable canine companions to her insights on blending emotions and mystery, Lucinda's journey is as captivating as the books she creates. It's a privilege to share her thoughts and experiences with our readers, and we think you'll agree—her stories leave an indelible mark on the heart.

What inspired you to blend paranormal elements with cozy mysteries in your Book Store Cozy Mystery series?

I love reading paranormal cozy mysteries, and adding those elements gives an author a broader license for creativity.

How do you balance the sweet, clean romance themes with suspenseful murder plots in your writing?

I would like to have anyone at any age read these books so keeping them sweet in the romance department and non-violent despite they're murder mystery books is the best avenue to success.

Which of your fictional characters do you personally relate to the most, and why?

Milo, the talking familiar, is fashioned after our former family cat, Mordy. I could always picture Mordy talking in a snarky but loving attitude.

How does living in western Massachusetts influence the small-town settings in your books?

Small town life means you recognize faces, family names and gasp, "you heard he did what?" kind of thing. Small towns are mini universe until themselves which again adds to the gasp factor in cozy mystery books.

What challenges have you faced transitioning from nonfiction writing to fiction?

Writing fiction is so much easier. :) I can have characters to what I want, say and act according to my muse. Its a wonderful thing. Non-fiction, is based in facts and its difficult to make technical documents interesting. There's no room for humor.

How do you develop the emotional depth in your later-in-life romance stories like Lost and Found?

I'm an older woman who has been blessed to experience love a second time. My personal life had "all the feels" and I wanted to bring that to life in my work.

Can you share your process for building series arcs that allow each book to also stand alone?

Elements connect the books as the series, such as family dynamics and the small town the books take place in. However, I try to write a book that has a satisfactory story arc of its own. But, getting to know the other characters provides depth to the reading experience.

Which book or series was the most fun for

Lucinda Race's storytelling captivates with warmth, humor, and imaginative tales, making her a cherished voice in romance and cozy mysteries.

you to write and what made it special?

That's like asking which is my favorite child. They're all special. For romance, I loved writing Price Family Romance Series. It was a spinoff from Ready to Soar and set in a winery in the Finger Lakes region of New York. My husband and I traveled there with friends and it was so enjoyable, it made the perfect setting for this series. And a new book in that series will be released in 2026. Stella Maxwell is finally getting her happily ever after.

How do you keep your ideas fresh after writing so many series and standalone novels?

Prior to becoming a full-time writer, I traveled for my day job. Sitting in airports and at conventions I was fortunate to observe people, and I always made up little stories about them, where did they live, family, dating, spouses, career choices, that kind of thing. I let my imagination come out to play and stories simmered. I have a pretty good memory so recall to certain locations, people and emotions come back when I'm ready to write them.

What advice would you give to aspiring authors who want to craft both mystery and romance into their stories?

Don't let what the rules say you can and can't do. For a long time I thought I couldn't write cozy and cross over since I was a romance author. But when I tossed away the rule book my creativity was unleashed. Just write what your muse is urging you to write. I promise, it's liberating.

Lucinda Race, surrounded by inspiration, pens heartwarming tales in the hills of western Massachusetts.

> *I love reading paranormal cozy mysteries, and adding those elements gives an author a broader license for creativity."*

Lucinda Race

Embrace Balance Wellness And Inner Peace Through Ancient Practice

Discover The Transformative Power Of Yoga For Mind Body And Soul

Yoga unites mind, body, and soul, offering physical health, mental clarity, and spiritual growth, making it accessible and transformative for everyone.

By Mosaic Digest Staff

In a world that often feels chaotic and fast-paced, yoga stands as a timeless sanctuary—a practice that has nurtured humanity for thousands of years. Originating in ancient India, yoga has transcended cultural and geographical boundaries to become a global phenomenon. This holistic discipline offers much more than physical exercise; it is a pathway to harmony, mindfulness, and self-discovery.

Yoga brings harmony, strength, and serenity, enriching lives with its timeless wisdom and gentle guidance toward holistic well-being.

THE ESSENCE OF YOGA

At its core, yoga is a union—a connection between the mind, body, and spirit. Derived from the Sanskrit word "yuj," meaning to yoke or unite, yoga integrates breathing techniques (pranayama), physical postures (asanas), and meditation to create a balanced lifestyle. It is not merely a workout but a way of life that fosters inner peace and resilience.

PHYSICAL BENEFITS

Yoga is renowned for its ability to enhance physical health. Regular practice improves flexibility, strength, and posture. Asanas like downward dog, warrior pose, and tree pose engage multiple muscle groups, promoting overall fitness. Moreover, yoga can alleviate chronic pain, boost immunity, and support cardiovascular health. The gentle yet profound movements make it accessible to individuals of all ages and fitness levels.

MENTAL CLARITY AND EMOTIONAL WELL-BEING

In a world filled with distractions, yoga offers a space to quiet the mind and cultivate mindfulness. Focused breathing and meditation practices reduce stress, anxiety, and depression, fostering emotional stability. Yoga encourages self-awareness, helping practitioners navigate life's challenges with grace and equanimity.

SPIRITUAL AWAKENING

Beyond the physical and mental realms, yoga delves into the spiritual. It invites individuals to explore their inner selves, connecting with their true nature. Practices like mantra chanting, visualization, and deep meditation awaken a sense of purpose and unity with the universe.

YOGA FOR EVERYONE

One of the most beautiful aspects of yoga is its inclusivity. Whether you're a seasoned practitioner or a beginner, yoga adapts to meet your needs. From gentle restorative yoga to dynamic vinyasa flows, there's a style for everyone. It's not about perfection but about showing up for yourself, one breath at a time.

INCORPORATING YOGA INTO DAILY LIFE

You don't need a yoga mat or a dedicated studio to embrace this practice. Simple acts like mindful breathing, body stretches, or a few moments of meditation can seamlessly integrate yoga into your daily routine. Start small, and let the practice evolve organically.

Yoga is more than a trend; it's a timeless gift to humanity. It empowers individuals to lead healthier, more mindful lives while fostering a deep connection with themselves and the world around them. Whether you're seeking physical strength, mental clarity, or spiritual growth, yoga offers a transformative journey. So, roll out your mat, take a deep breath, and embark on this beautiful path of self-discovery. Namaste.

Photo: A peaceful yoga session under golden sunlight, embodying calm and balance.

Blending Real-Life Experiences with Magic and Meaning

Alexis Anicque shares her sailing-inspired adventures, the magic of storytelling, and the importance of courage, creativity, and living life without regrets in this engaging and insightful conversation.

Alexis Anicque Inspires Readers Through Adventure, Courage, and Authentic Storytelling

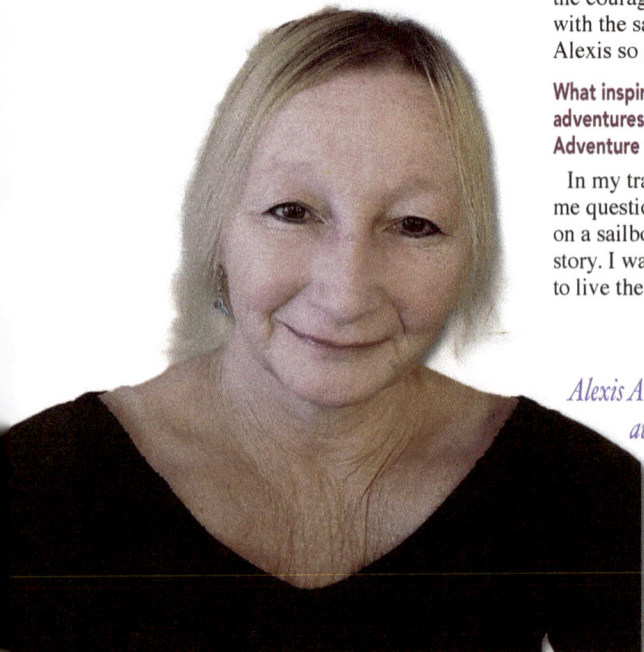

Alexis Anicque embodies the spirit of adventure, creativity, and the courage to live life on her terms, and *Mosaic Digest* magazine is thrilled to feature her in this exclusive interview. As an accomplished author, devoted wife, mother, and vibrant world traveler, Alexis is the kind of storyteller whose passion leaps off the pages. Whether sailing the open seas, crafting fantastical worlds, or penning heartfelt reflections inspired by her adventurous life, Alexis has an unparalleled gift for drawing readers into deeply authentic narratives.

From her riveting non-fiction series "*Our Alternative Lifestyle Adventure Stories,*" which offers an inspiring glimpse into life aboard a sailboat, to her enchanting novels like "Finding Famous," blending fantasy and self-discovery, Alexis Ancique demonstrates an extraordinary ability to not only entertain but also move her readers profoundly. Her boldness, resilience, and love of living in the moment serve as a beacon for us all to chase our dreams without fear of failure.

Mosaic Digest is honored to celebrate both Alexis's literary artistry and her power to ignite the imagination and ambition of her audience. As you read her candid responses in this interview, we hope you discover not just the depth behind her stories but also the courage to pursue your own passions with the same adventurous spirit that makes Alexis so remarkable.

What inspired you to share your real-life sailing adventures in the "Our Alternative Lifestyle Adventure Stories" series?

In my travels I had so many people asking me questions about what life was like living on a sailboat. It truly inspired me to tell my story. I wanted to be an inspiration for others to live their dreams.

Alexis Anicque: Adventurer, storyteller, and author inspiring others to live boldly and embrace the extraordinary moments life offers.

How did your own experiences living on a boat shape the tone and authenticity of your writing?

Living on a sailboat is a great challenge and forces you to think outside of the norm. It also gives you plenty of time to read and enjoy life away from the TV, internet, and electronics that cloud your imagination.

In "Finding Famous", what drew you to blend elements of fantasy and self-discovery in the storyline?

Honestly, it started out to be a heartfelt journey of a mother and daughter, but I got bored with the story and had to change everything after I added magic to the journal. I still wanted to touch the readers, but also entertain them as well.

Do you find it challenging to switch between writing fiction and non-fiction, and how do you balance the two?

I actually just love telling stories whether they are true or not so I write what I'm feeling about at the time. I cannot imagine limiting myself to one or the other.

Which of your characters do you feel most connected to, and why?

Definitely Vanessa in "From Money to Murder" because I based her personality on mine.

How do your travels and love for adventure influence your storytelling process?

I truly enjoy sharing my experiences with others, which is why I write the places and experiences in all of my books.

What message do you hope readers take away from your books about courage and following one's dreams?

I think I said it best in "Jump Before You Fall" . You never know if you will be able to get up again. Life is so fleeting and I hope I help others to choose not to have regrets and take opportunities to live every moment.

What advice would you give to aspiring authors who wish to write authentically from their own life experiences?

In this day and age the route of traditional publishing is out of reach for most. I say, tell your story, make sure it is publish ready, and self publish. Never let those naysayers stop you from telling your story.self publish. Never let those naysayers stop you from telling your story.

"

Living on a sailboat is a great challenge and forces you to think outside of the norm.

Alexis Anicque

D anica Dakić, a visionary artist whose work has been profoundly shaped by her experiences during the Bosnian War and the siege of Sarajevo, continues to captivate audiences with her exploration of identity, collectivity, and the interplay between personal and public narratives. An interview conducted with the artist for Mosaic Digest delves into the transformative impact of these experiences on her artistic vision and practice.

The war in Bosnia and the subsequent isolation from her homeland marked a pivotal shift in Dakić's artistic journey. During this period, she grappled with the meaning and function of art, leading her to explore new themes, media, and methods. Her installation "Blaues Auge" (1996) exemplifies this shift, addressing the disconnection between personal experience and media narratives. By collaging thousands of newspaper photos and headlines on transparent foil, Dakić created a powerful visual barrier that symbolized the opacity of media representations during times of conflict. This work, and others like it, reflect her ongoing artistic engagement with the tension between personal and public narratives.

Dakić's video installation "Grand Organ" (2010), commissioned for the Touched exhibition at St. George's Hall in Liverpool, further exemplifies her innovative approach to art. Inspired by the hall's majestic organ and neoclassical architecture, the installation explores themes of justice, performance, and music. By transforming the boys' choir into an organ with human pipe voices, composer Bojan Vuletić's sound design highlights the interplay between the legal system and spectacle. The involvement of local choirs, including the Liverpool Signing Choir and the "Sparrows" of Sparrow Hall, underscores Dakić's focus on polyphony and childhood, creating a narrative that examines power dynamics and community.

Throughout her career, Dakić has experimented with various mediums, from painting to video, sound, and text. Her choice of medium is driven by the narrative or message she wishes to convey, with each medium offering a unique way to experience her images. As an "image maker," Dakić believes in the power of images to communicate complex ideas and emotions that transcend traditional media boundaries.

Dakić's work is deeply informed by historical and social contexts, particularly in relation to identity and collectivity. While her personal experiences of war and displacement influence her exploration of these themes, her art speaks to universal experiences of mobility, migration, and living in multiple languages and cultures. Her work invites viewers to reflect on the perception of the global present and the role of the individual within larger societal structures.

The tension between individuality and collectivity is a recurring theme in Dakić's art, as seen in the allegorical references to music and law in "Grand Organ." She explores this tension on visual, acoustic, performative, and emotional levels, offering a nuanced perspective on the individual's place within society. Her art challenges viewers to consider the complexities of identity and the interconnectedness of personal and collective experiences.

Danica Dakić's artistic journey is a testament to her resilience and creativity in the face of adversity. Her work continues to inspire and provoke thought, offering a powerful commentary on the human condition and the ever-evolving narratives that shape our world. Through her innovative use of media and exploration of profound themes, Dakić has established herself as a leading voice in contemporary art, captivating audiences with her ability to transform personal experiences into universal narratives.

Art as a Bridge Between Personal and Public Narratives

Danica Dakić discusses how the Bosnian War influenced her art, exploring themes of identity, collectivity, and the tension between personal and public narratives through innovative media.

> Dakić's experiences during the Bosnian War reshaped her artistic vision, leading to new themes and media explorations.

Art & Culture

Danica Dakić is a visionary artist whose profound insights and creativity transform personal experiences into universal narratives.

" *The war had a strong influence on my life and my art.*"

Danica Dakić

The Art of Simplicity:
Perry Offer's Blueprint for Business Success

BY MOSAIC DIGEST STAFF

Photo: *Perry Offer in action, leading the charge for innovation and success at Wood Hosiery with a focus on simplicity and strategic growth.*

Harnessing Simplicity to Revolutionize the Business Landscape

Perry Offer discusses his philosophy of simplicity in business, outlining how it transformed Wood Hosiery into a market leader while fostering resilience and adaptability to overcome modern challenges in the corporate environment.

Perry Offer stands out as a beacon of clarity in the often chaotic world of business. Known for his transformative influence on companies struggling to navigate complexity, he has forged a remarkable career based on the guiding principle that simplicity is essential for success. Through his own experiences—shaped by personal challenges and professional triumphs—Perry has developed a unique approach that resonates with entrepreneurs and seasoned business leaders alike.

From an early age, Perry faced significant adversity. His father's sudden departure when he was just six years old instilled in him a deep sense of resilience and independence. "As a child, I didn't dwell on my family situation; my instinct was to ensure my own survival," Perry recalls. This formative experience laid the groundwork for his business ethos: a commitment to facing challenges directly and adapting to change without hesitation. "You cannot ignore problems when they arise. Instead, you must confront them, prepare for the inevitable changes, and push forward," he asserts.

Perry's perspective on business takes shape during his tenure at Wood Hosiery. At the age of 22, he took on the role of Director of Finance for a company that was thriving but beginning to stagnate. "We understood that stagnation could quickly lead to decline, and decisive action was necessary," he reflects. His research and analysis revealed a unique opportunity to streamline operations. Rather than continuing to produce tights solely to order—resulting in lengthy delivery times—Perry spearheaded a change in production strategy. By maintaining a large stock of white tights that could be dyed as needed, he significantly reduced delivery times from weeks to mere days. This innovative shift helped Wood Hosiery soar to prominence, eventually producing a million pairs of tights each week.

The success of Wood Hosiery became a testament to Perry's belief that a clear focus can lead to profound improvements. "We learned how to enhance profitability and service without compromising our existing strengths," he explains. This principle of simplifying processes while honing in on core objectives has become a hallmark of Perry's consultancy work across a variety of industries.

As Perry ventured beyond individual companies, he emerged as a vocal critic of the wider business landscape in the UK. He attributes the struggles faced by many businesses to excessive complexity and mismanagement. "Excessive regulation and bureaucracy stifle innovation," he argues, highlighting a growing concern in an increasingly convoluted regulatory environment. Perry's advocacy for simplicity extends to both business leaders and policymakers, urging them to eliminate obstacles that hinder progress. "Take a step back, assess your operations, and you will quickly identify inefficiencies that complicate your business," he advises.

Perry also stresses the importance of pers-

Perry Offer is a dynamic leader who embodies innovation, inspiring others with his vision and dedication to making businesses thrive through simplicity and efficiency.

---

pective when navigating the complexities of modern commerce. He encourages leaders to regard technology—such as artificial intelligence—not as a panacea but as a tool to enhance operations without adding confusion. "When technology is treated merely as a tool rather than as a team member, it can complicate rather than simplify," he cautions. This view plays a vital role in an era where reliance on technology can sometimes create more challenges than solutions.

With years of experience advising businesses of all sizes, Perry has identified a common pitfall: the tendency to seek incremental changes within already complicated systems. "Making minor adjustments to address complex issues does not solve the problem; it simply adds more layers to an already tangled web," he states. Instead, he urges businesses to embrace simplification as a core principle. "When faced with a crisis, streamline your strategy, eliminate what's not working, and return to the essentials." This mantra is applicable across the board, regardless of whether a company is a small startup or a large corporation.

Perry's insights are particularly timely in the current global landscape, which is rife with rapid change and uncertainty. He encourages business leaders to stay focused on their fundamental missions, resisting distractions that could lead them astray. "Opportunities might feel fleeting, but do not abandon a good idea simply because it presents challenges," he insists. "If your vision remains valid, it might just be your approach that needs refining, with simplification as your guiding principle."

In discussing contemporary threats to businesses, Perry points to the financial instability of governments and the resulting political upheaval. "The potential bankruptcy of governments and an unstable geopolitical environment pose significant challenges," he warns. Addressing these broader threats requires businesses to maintain adaptability and resilience while embracing a strategy rooted in simplicity.

Additionally, Perry has tackled the impact of political correctness on innovation, arguing that excessive regulation can burden businesses. He likens such regulations to weights that hinder a runner's speed. "The critical question is, who will prevail: the runner bogged down by complexity or the one who is streamlined and focused?" he muses. He believes that many businesses have become ensnared in systems that, while well-intentioned, obscure their original goals and hinder their potential.

For startups and new ventures, Perry outlines three guiding principles intended to foster success while maintaining simplicity: First, concentrate on a specific niche, ensuring that capturing even a small percentage of demand can yield considerable returns. Second, identify the key feature of your product or service that will resonate most with your target audience. Finally, focus intensively on consistently delivering that core value, and when you achieve your goals, be ready to pivot toward new challenges.

Perry's commitment to simplicity is not just a practical business strategy; it embodies a deeper philosophy that brings clarity in dif-

---

"Don't let AI become more important than a tool—it's not a staff member."
– Perry Offer

"Simplicity is the only way forward."
– Perry Offer

---

ficult times. Both aspiring entrepreneurs and experienced executives can learn valuable lessons from his journey. In today's marketplace, success tends to favour leaders who can navigate through chaos and maintain a focus on what truly matters.

Looking to the future, the assertion is clear: The case for simplicity in business has never been more urgent. Perry Offer's insights remind us that in an age marked by distractions and uncertainties, having a clear purpose and a dedication to simplifying operations can pave the way for sustained success. It is those who dare to embrace simplicity in a complex world who are poised to emerge as leaders, guiding their businesses toward new heights in an ever-evolving global landscape.

For Perry Offer, simplicity is more than just a method; it is a philosophy capable of transforming organisations and redefining industries. By adopting this mindset, business leaders can navigate today's challenges and seize opportunities for tomorrow. As Perry succinctly puts it, "In times of chaos, having the courage to simplify can be the most revolutionary act of all."

L.E. Summers Shares Wisdom on Dementia Caregiving Through Compassion and Experience

BY MOSAIC DIGEST STAFF

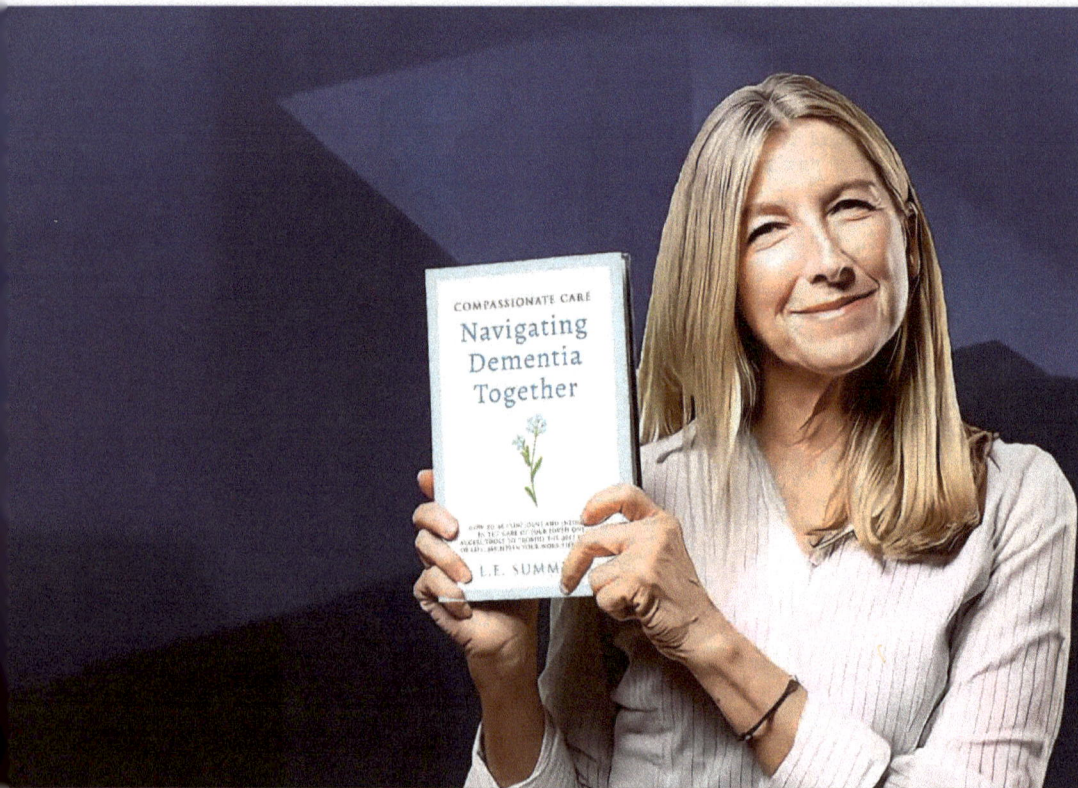

Photo: *"Compassionate Care: Navigating Dementia Together" by L.E. Summers offers a comprehensive guide for caregivers, providing practical tools, emotional support, and actionable steps to confidently care for loved ones with dementia while prioritizing self-care.*

A Former IT Professional Turned Author Offers Practical Guidance and Emotional Support for Caregivers

L.E. Summers, a former IT professional turned dementia caregiving expert, shares their journey, practical advice, and heartfelt insights to help caregivers navigate challenges while prioritizing their own well-being.

L.E. Summers is a beacon of hope and guidance for caregivers navigating the often overwhelming journey of dementia care. With a trilogy of insightful books—*Compassionate Care: Navigating Dementia Together, Compassionate Care: A Practical Handbook for Dementia Caregiving,* and *Compassionate Care: Accepting the Dementia Diagnosis*—Summers offers both practical advice and emotional support to those tending to loved ones with dementia. Drawing from personal experience as a caregiver for their mother, Summers' work is a testament to resilience, compassion, and the power of shared knowledge. Their dedication to helping caregivers maintain their own well-being while providing tender care is both inspiring and invaluable.

Here at *Mosaic Digest*, we are honored to feature L.E. Summers in this heartfelt interview, where they share their journey, insights, and the profound lessons learned along the way. Their story is a reminder that even in the face of immense challenges, understanding and empathy can light the path forward.

What inspired you to write about your caregiving experience with your mother who had dementia?

I started on my dementia caregiving journey during the COVID outbreak. My sister was expecting her first grandchild. As health concerns dominated the early days of 2020, I became the natural choice for caregiving for my mother. I had just retired as an IT professional and earned a real estate license. I traveled 1,600 miles from my home to once again sleep in my bedroom from age 11. On my first day of care, my mom's doctor wanted to meet with me to discuss hospice care. I vowed to keep up the fight to ensure that my mother got to meet her first great-grandchild. This was never a path that I anticipated for myself, but it taught me so much about growing old, family, love, and perseverance. I struggled at first, but I kept notes on what

> *"Find new ways to communicate and cherish the times together, even when they seem so different from earlier times."*

worked and what didn't. I couldn't find much information on dementia and caregiving. With my books, I am sharing my notes, my experience, and writing what I wish I had found but didn't.

How do you think your books can help alleviate the feelings of isolation and uncertainty that many caregivers face?

Caregiving can make you feel incredibly isolated, especially when you are making decisions about someone you love while watching them change before your eyes. With my books I hope to provide practical guidance and emotional validation. Reading reviews of my books, I see that they help people like me feel less alone. When you question yourself about whether you are doing enough or doing the right thing, having a book that tells you "this is normal, and here is what helps" is incredibly reassuring.

L.E. Summers' compassionate, firsthand expertise provides invaluable guidance, empowering caregivers with practical solutions and emotional reassurance in their toughest moments.

Can you discuss the importance of prioritizing one's own wellbeing whilst caring for a loved one with dementia?

As a caregiver, you must learn that you cannot sacrifice yourself and still be effective. Neglecting your own well-being makes you a depleted caregiver. You cannot provide compassionate care when you are stressed and running on empty. In my books, practical self-care is emphasized. You need a backup, directly in caregiving and indirectly in the day-to-day requirements in your own life. I embraced meditation and found great benefit in my 15-minute "vacations."

How do you think the DICE model can be applied in real-life caregiving situations?

The DICE model helped me in resolving issues that seemed too challenging for me. Describe, Investigate, Create, Evaluate serves to break down behaviors and discover potential triggers. Are they hungry, tired, in pain? By taking a logical approach, trial and error can avoid chaos. It became a sort of toolkit for me. My notebook was filled with my experiments and what worked and what to avoid.

What role do you believe support networks play in the caregiving journey?

There is no question that support networks are essential. Support comes in various ways and tiers. It is about finding the right people for different needs. Practical support like grocery shopping or picking up medications is invaluable. Others can support you and your loved one emotionally. It is important to express to others the specific support that you need and let them provide that help. In my books, I help identify, build and maintain these critical support systems. Online support from groups like the Alzheimer's Association and local hospital groups provide a wealth of information for no charge at all. Faith groups are a true gift to caregivers.

How did you find the process of writing a Spanish edition of your first book, and what prompted you to do so?

My own upbringing was immersed in the Hispanic community. When a fellow author offered to translate my first book into Spanish, it felt like a natural progression. Of course, the Hispanic community has the same struggles with dementia and caregiving. The language barriers can make an already challenging situation even more isolating. It is always best to navigate challenges without dealing with language differences. I found so little available for caregivers in Spanish. I hope to translate my other books soon.

What do you hope readers take away from your series of books on caregiving and dementia?

Ideally, I want readers of my books to feel less isolated and more confident in their caregiving responsibilities. There is no map, and often they wonder if their decisions are the right ones. I want them not to feel that they are failing when things don't seem to be working. Trial and error is key. I offer suggestions and encouragement. Self-care is so important. Their loved one cannot drink from an empty cup. Find new ways to communicate and cherish the times together, even when they seem so different from earlier times.

What advice would you give to fellow authors who are considering writing about their experiences with caregiving or dementia?

Write from your heart. Share your practical experience. Your authority comes from what you have learned. I have no certificate to provide medical advice, but I do have what I have learned, and I want to share that. I feel that my readers appreciate the authenticity and compassion that I offer. Remember that your perspective is unique, but it is still relevant to others. Your story matters!

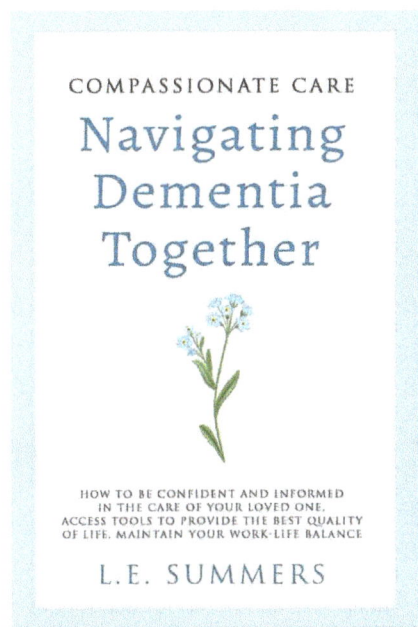

COMPASSIONATE CARE

Navigating Dementia Together

HOW TO BE CONFIDENT AND INFORMED
IN THE CARE OF YOUR LOVED ONE.
ACCESS TOOLS TO PROVIDE THE BEST QUALITY
OF LIFE. MAINTAIN YOUR WORK-LIFE BALANCE

L.E. SUMMERS

"Compassionate Care: Navigating Dementia Together" is an invaluable guide for caregivers, offering practical advice, emotional support, and actionable steps. L.E. Summers provides clear strategies for managing dementia's challenges while prioritizing self-care. Highly rated and deeply empathetic, this book is a must-read for anyone supporting a loved one with dementia.

Paula Minydzak Shares Insights On Crafting Stories Rooted In Heritage And Crime Fiction

BY MOSAIC DIGEST STAFF

Photo: *Paula Minydzak, author of The Firstborn Son and The Second Son, merging heritage and suspense in captivating fiction.*

A Blend Of Heritage And Suspense

Paula Minydzak discusses her writing journey, heritage-inspired characters, genre shifts, crime research, and creative process, while offering advice to emerging authors on crafting personal yet compelling narratives.

Paula Minydzak, an author of remarkable talent and an incredible storyteller, captivates readers through her exploration of identity, family, and suspense—all woven with vivid threads of Pittsburgh heritage and Italian-Slovak traditions. Combining her unique voice with rich personal experiences, Paula crafts narratives that resonate deeply, balancing intrigue, emotion, and authenticity. From her award-nominated debut *The Firstborn Son* to her thrilling new crime fiction novel *The Second Son*, Paula showcases her gift for drawing readers into layered worlds filled with moral dilemmas, familial loyalties, and riveting suspense.

Mosaic Digest is thrilled to present an exclusive interview with Paula Minydzak, whose work exemplifies the best of contemporary fiction. With her legal and technical background, and professional tailoring for film, Paula's diverse skill set and unforgettable characters add unparalleled depth to her storytelling. Her ability to transform personal heritage into compelling plots and relatable struggles leaves an indelible mark on readers, proving her mastery across genres. As you read this interview, you'll discover how Paula's relentless passion, creative reinvention, and dedication to craft shape the powerful stories that distinguish her as a rising star in fiction. Mosaic Digest is honored to feature Paula Minydzak—the voice behind gripping, heartfelt tales that continue to inspire.

Your debut novel, The Firstborn Son, was a finalist in the NJ Romance Writers Best First Book category in 2023. How did that recognition shape your confidence and approach as a writer?

Knowing that the NJ Romance Writers contest was generally well-attended, I felt like I had achieved a particular writing goal: maintaining a reader's interest with quality writing. It encouraged me to write more and stretch beyond a single genre.

You've transitioned from writing romance to suspense. What prompted that shift, and how has your creative process adapted to the change in genre?

When I originally wrote The Firstborn Son, the publisher wanted it to have graphic sex scenes. As I added them into the novel, I found that I did not enjoy writing that level of heat. I think long sex scenes pull a reader out of the story. So, when I wrote the Second Son and published it myself, I used romance as a sideline rather than the main event.

Pittsburgh, your hometown, and your Italian and Slovak heritage seem to feature in your storytelling. How do these roots influence your characters and settings?

I grew up in a close-knit family whose bonds were strengthened through life experiences. I found that my family was similar to other Italian families. It lends credibility to my writing. The Slovak side offered a contrast.

Pittsburgh was known for the steel industry that put immigrants to work in the late 1800s and early 1900s, then suffered the loss of that industry in later decades. I was sixteen when mass unemployment plunged every family into hardship.

> Paula Minydzak is a brilliant story-teller whose authenticity, genre versatility, and ability to create heartfelt characters are truly inspiring.

You have experience as a tailor and patternmaker and even did costuming work for films. In what ways does that background inform your descriptive writing or character wardrobe details?

Costuming made me aware of historic styles, fabrics and how they perform. So I might write about a silk dress that flutters when someone spins around, or a bias cut that naturally clings to the figure regardless of the fabric type. When I wrote both of my novels, I continually imagined what the costumes would look like in film.

Your new novel, The Second Son, dives into crime fiction and suspense. What research did you undertake to ensure authenticity in the world of money laundering and mafia rivalries?

Somewhere around 1925, supposedly the mafia tried to recruit my Italian grandfather, but he assumed they would use his wife and children to manipulate him and stayed away. I combined that history with what I imagined was correct about mafia films and other mafia novels. The money laundering knowledge comes from my day job for a global bank and knowing that all banks must follow certain laws. The fight scenes came from talking to my brother about boxing and from some martial arts classes I had years ago. I find that credibility in fight scenes is hard to master.

In The Second Son, Joey Renzi is torn between family loyalty and personal ethics. How do you balance portraying the emotional weight of his dilemma while keeping the plot tight and compelling?

Joey's character was forced to create his own moral code because he did not subscribe to his father's lifestyle. The code seeps into each decision he makes, but he must continually think, then act and work around his emotions. To drive the quick pace, I did not give Joey too much time to deliberate.

Your protagonist's struggle with past identity—as seen in Joey's efforts to escape the shadow of his enforcer past—is deeply personal. Do you draw from your own experiences with reinvention or family expectations?

After I struggled with a harsh personal issue in my early 20s, I learned that one lives with some things for a lifetime. Unforgettable experiences can mold a person through shame or triumph, through disappointment or hope.

You mention engaging workshops and personalised writing assistance, including beta-read exchanges. How have these collaborations influenced your revision process or storytelling finesse?

I perfected my speaking skills at my day job, so I created workshops on topics that can help other writers, such as financial crimes or the makings of a good presentation. Manuscript exchanges are more of a learning experience for me, whereby someone can tell me how to improve. By reading another author's novel, I often think of questions that are not answered, characters that are not fully developed, or what I might do to increase the pace. This awareness helps me correct my own writing.

Your Norwegian Elkhound, Boss, shares your home in Pittsburgh. Is there a story or scene in your writing that Boss inspired, even in a subtle or serendipitous way?

Boss is extremely protective and vocal, and I often imagine what he wants to tell me. The cat in The Second Son acts as though Boss would in many situations.

Finally, what advice would you offer to emerging authors who are contemplating a genre shift—perhaps from romance to suspense—or who wish to integrate elements of their personal heritage into their fiction?

Write something you can be proud of and worry about genre later. We are experts at how our lives are fashioned, by what we feel or do, by our dreams and failures. This is the stuff great characters are made of. I believe all good books start with an author who could star in the main role.

Erotokritos Z. Kalogeratos Inspires With Riveting Tales Of Hope And Thrilling Geopolitical Insights

BY MOSAIC DIGEST STAFF

Photo: *Erotokritos Z. Kalogeratos: Adventurer, Analyst, Storyteller Extraordinaire*

A Visionary Worldbuilder Crafting Hope Through Fiction

Erotokritos Z. Kalogeratos weaves worlds of hope and thrill, blending Greek folklore, geopolitical insights, and adventure into fast-paced, cinematic stories like The King of Black and The Irish Mist.

Erotokritos Z. Kalogeratos is a literary force who seamlessly bridges the realms of gripping fiction and sharp geopolitical analysis. His body of work is as diverse as his life story—a tapestry woven with the threads of adventure, intellect, and humanity. From serving in the Greek Special Forces to crafting intricate, deeply symbolic worlds set in the aftermath of civilization's collapse, Kalogeratos is the modern Renaissance man we never knew we needed. His books, like *The King of Black*, offer readers more than just escapism; they present a vision of hope and rebirth, allowing us to confront the darkness while believing in the inevitability of light.

But Kalogeratos's brilliance doesn't end with speculative fiction. His expertise as a geopolitical analyst enriches his writing with strategic nuance, while his early ventures into spy adventures, like *The Irish Mist*, showcase his versatility. What sets him apart is the authenticity rooted in his diverse experiences—whether navigating the Mediterranean as a merchant mariner or speaking three languages fluently, his characters breathe with a realism only life itself can lend.

With his rich use of Greek folklore and vivid descriptions of the Ionian Islands, Kalogeratos anchors his stories in timeless truths and vibrant imaginations. As he builds thrilling universes that span the spectrum between dystopian fantasy and hard geopolitical commentary, Kalogeratos emerges not merely as an author but as a storyteller capable of reshaping perspectives.

At *Mosaic Digest Magazine,* we are honored to have had the privilege of hearing from Erotokritos Z. Kalogeratos—a man whose stories challenge, inspire, and motivate us to think beyond the boundaries of tradition and complacency. We hope you enjoy diving into this exclusive interview, where Kalogeratos shares his motivations, creative process, and his belief that hope is the one force capable of renewing the world. With much more on the horizon, this is an author whose journey will spark conversations across continents and generations.

What inspired you to create a world set 230 "cycles" after the collapse of civilization—a world both haunting and thrilling?

I believe, that what makes the world go round is hope! And in the times, we live in there is very little of it. So, I thought I would look past the bad things we all fear might come and fast-forward to that moment when hope begins to grow again, gradually taking over the world. The "King of Black," Lokros, symbolizes this hope, while the closed community of the small, anonymous island represents the concept of family, from which hope will be reborn. Besides, crafting my own universe where I could control every detail—the characters, the rules, the endings, thus, creating a "new world" is relatively easy—I admit it. When writing that, you have the freedom to shape whatever you want, unconstrained by reality.

Your writing life seems infused with adventure and struggle. How do your real-life experiences influence your storytelling?

Very much so! I believe life is a constant struggle—and I don't find that stressful at

---

Erotokritos Z. Kalogeratos is a master creator who transforms reality, mythology, and imagination into timeless, thought-provoking literary treasures.

---

all. On the contrary, it's exhilarating to keep moving, to change your environment, to face new challenges. My storytelling is fast-paced and cinematic—it doesn't wait. The same goes for my life. I've worked in completely different environments and rarely hesitated to make a fresh start, even if it was the opposite of what I'd done before.

You reference Greek names, locations, and folklore. Is there deeper symbolism, or is it simply something you're comfortable with?

Both, actually. Our civilization, which now seems to be fading, has deep roots in Greece. I thought it logical and fitting that the next one—the world in The King of Black—should also draw from that same well. And yes, you're right: writing about my homeland, the Ionian Islands, feels natural. It's easier to create the "island with no name" because I've visited such places in real life.

Why King of Black? What's the significance of the title?

Well, It has nothing to do with old movies or anything like that. In a simple, post-modern world, I imagined concepts would also be straightforward, simple and functional. There's the Oligarch of Red, which perfectly

captures that faction's mentality—simple, bold: red. The same goes for the Oligarch of Yellow. My protagonist, however, didn't belong to the rulers but to the ruled. His color is more subdued, less cheerful: black.

What about the rest of your work? I've noticed geopolitical analysis eBooks that diverge completely from your fictional worlds, dealing with hard reality.

That stems from my current job as a political and geopolitical analyst. I write essays for three international websites and two of my own, and I advise two politicians currently in office. When I feel a topic needs emphasis, I compile a short eBook. I have too many such essays—only a fraction is published. The Eastern Mediterranean fascinates me deeply, both as a Greek and because it's been the "heart" of major geopolitical conflicts for centuries.

What about your spy adventure eBook, The Irish Mist, about the IRA?

That was my first attempt at writing. I typed it on a small red Royal typewriter around 1984. The IRA's struggle always fascinated me—the passionate desire for self-determination, even when the oppressor shares so much with the oppressed, as with Britain and Ireland. Of course, I don't condone terrorism, but I understand the yearning for freedom. Greeks felt the same during centuries of Ottoman occupation, never ceasing to fight until we won our freedom. Also, I've always been intrigued by "lone wolf" heroes like Tarloch, the protagonist. His character is based on a real Greek officer who undertook secret missions.

What can we expect from you next? What are you working on now?

I'm deeply immersed in the King of Black series, which will span several more books. Lokros's world will explode and reshape itself—I hope readers find it as thrilling as I do.

What advice would you give other authors seeking to build a sustainable and imaginative writing career?

Sorry, I do not believe in giving advices—except perhaps, to follow what your heart insists on, even if your mind resists. I write because I need to run, escape, build, and destroy. I write hoping others will join me, inspired to write about their own worlds, dreams, and realities. I wish everyone charming, mysterious, and adventurous journeys through the pages of a book.

Thank you for this interview, from the bottom of my heart. Lokros sends his thanks as well...

Tim Grove Brings History To Life Through Engaging Adventures And Intriguing Past Narratives

BY MOSAIC DIGEST STAFF

Photo: *Tim Grove, Inspiring Historian And Acclaimed Author Of Award-Winning Nonfiction Books For Young Readers*

Passion For History And Storytelling | Award-Winning Author Of Nonfiction For Young Readers

Tim Grove discusses his journey as an author and public historian, highlighting his unique approach to writing engaging history-based nonfiction for younger audiences while preserving historical accuracy and depth.

Tim Grove is a name synonymous with passion for history and a remarkable ability to bring the richness of the past to life for audiences young and old. As a distinguished author, historian, and educator, Tim has carved a unique niche in the literary and historical world by demonstrating the profound relevance of history in our daily lives. His books, award-winning and celebrated, explore diverse topics—from breathtaking adventures in aviation to pivotal moments in civil rights—all while balancing rigorous historical accuracy with captivating narrative appeal. It is this artful balance that has made his works invaluable resources for educators and enthralling reads for young learners.

At Mosaic Digest magazine, we celebrate storytellers like Tim Grove who are redefining how history is experienced and understood. Through his career spanning two and a half decades, Tim has not only contributed to major institutions like the Smithsonian, but he has also profoundly impacted the field with his innovative approach to museum education and his ability to uncover the human stories behind historical events. His book *First Flight Around the World* illuminates the fascinating tale of courage and ambition in the race for global aviation supremacy, while his Yorktown book unearths the intriguing story of an enslaved spy during the American Revolution.

Tim's work exemplifies the idea that history isn't just a record of the past—it's a living narrative that speaks to who we are today. Mosaic Digest magazine is proud to feature an exclusive interview with Tim Grove in this issue, delving into his creative process, his fondest achievements, and his unwavering commitment to making history both accessible and essential for younger audiences. Whether through his engaging writing, his award-winning books, or his trailblazing contributions as a public historian, Tim reminds us that great stories, rooted in historical truth, have the power to inspire generations.

Your background as a public historian has led you

to work with institutions like the Smithsonian. How has this experience shaped your approach to writing nonfiction for young readers?

I think that by focusing on projects such as exhibitions and programs for public consumption, I have gained a strong sense of how to make history accessible and engaging to a broad spectrum of people. One aspect of public history shaping my writing is my desire to help people understand the historical process – how historians arrive at their conclusions based on primary evidence. In general I don't think the history field has done a good job of revealing the process, especially why history interpretations change. I've begun to try to shed light on this process in my writing.

My work on exhibitions has definitely generated book ideas. For example, when working on the Pioneers of Flight gallery at the National Air and Space Museum I became acquainted with the Douglas World Cruiser named Chicago, the first airplane around the world in 1924. Most Americans aren't aware of its story, a terrific adventure story. Obstacles aside, the story is even more captivating because it was a race for first among six

Tim Grove is a masterful historian and author whose books captivate readers and make history accessible, vibrant, and unforgettable.

nations. When I learned that the museum's archives held the journal of the plane's mechanic and many photos from the trip, I realized I was sitting on a treasure trove. It was the kind of story I wanted to read when I was a boy.

That book, "First Flight Around the World," captures a thrilling historical event. What drew you to this story, and what do you hope young readers take away from it?

As I mentioned above, it was a grand adventure, is well-documented, and was a race. Plus, it took place in a time of great change in the world – radio had just been invented, colonial powers still ruled large sections of the world but their control was diminishing. And airplanes had only been invented twenty-one years earlier. Many people around the world had never seen an airplane. The United States was not an air power and the army, which initiated the flight, wanted to prove to the world that it could compete in the air, especially since Americans invented the airplane. It helped me that my main source, the journal, was written by someone who could write, had a sense of humor, and included incidents such as encounters with new animals, that made the story more enticing for young readers.

From aviation to civil rights, your books cover a wide range of American history. What's the common thread you look for when choosing a topic to write about?

I choose diverse topics but first, no surprise, the topic must engage me enough to make me want to spend several years on the research and writing process. I don't necessarily shy away from well-known topics or topics that have been written about before, but there must be a new twist. For my Yorktown book, The World Turned Upside Down, about the last major campaign of the American Revolution, I learned of an enslaved man who became a spy for General Lafayette. I was immediately intrigued because that's a rare person. Obviously I had to do research to see if I could uncover enough of his story—if source materials existed. Enslaved people and spies were not typically leaving documentary evidence of their activities.

You've mentioned your passion for making history accessible and engaging. What techniques do you use to balance historical accuracy with narrative appeal?

For me it comes down to the source materials. Do they provide enough insight into my main characters? Are there quotes from them that I can weave into the narrative to make their voice authentic?

As an author with multiple accolades, including awards from the American Library Association and National Council for the Social Studies, what has been the most memorable moment or recognition in your writing career so far?

I was deeply honored that my first book for young readers, First Flight Around the World, was a finalist for the American Library Association's YALSA Excellence in nonfiction award.

What advice would you give aspiring nonfiction writers who want to bring history to life for younger audiences?

The more narrative style a nonfiction book can be, the better. What I mean is it should contain a story arc, character development, setting description, etc. -- elements of fiction writing. I try to include multiple points of view when possible – let the reader get into the head of several characters. Again it means knowing if the source materials will provide this point of view – is there a diary or court transcript or something else that will offer insight and direct quotes you can use? Since multiple perspectives are a foundation of historical thinking, this supports my desire to give readers some insight into the historical process. How do historians think and research? What questions do they ask? I also try to feature a variety of types of source materials – maps, documents, objects, oral history, photographs – to show the evidence that historians work with.

It's important to ask questions before you embark on a book project. Why do I think my audience will be attracted to this topic? Is there natural tension within the story? Are the characters likeable? Can I offer something new if the story has been written about before?

Christopher Miller Shares His Journey Of Heart-Centred Coaching And Strengths-Based Leadership

BY MOSAIC DIGEST STAFF

Photo: *Christopher Miller guiding others through heart-centred coaching while sharing his journey of love, resilience, and personal growth.*

Discover How Love, Resilience, And Purpose Can Transform Lives And Businesses Through Practical Wisdom And Insight

Christopher Miller blends personal experience, coaching expertise, and strengths-based strategies to guide readers toward fulfilment, love, and professional success, empowering them to integrate heart and purpose into every aspect of life.

Christopher Miller embodies the rare blend of intellect, heart, and purpose that defines truly transformative leaders. From his early roots in Canada to his global influence as a consultant, coach, and author, Christopher's journey has been guided by one central philosophy — living and leading with love. His ability to merge strategic business acumen with deep emotional intelligence has made him an inspiration to readers and professionals alike.

His acclaimed FISH series — beginning with The Joy of Finding FISH and continuing through Finding FISH in a Strengths-Based Practice — offers a roadmap to fulfilment, inspiration, success, and happiness. Through his writing and his Expansive.Love initiative, Christopher invites the world to embrace a more compassionate and heart-centred approach to life and work.

Christopher Miller inspires with practical guidance, heartfelt wisdom, and transformative insights that encourage readers to live fully and lead with authenticity.

Mosaic Digest magazine proudly features Christopher Miller in this insightful interview, where he shares his wisdom on balancing purpose and passion, navigating love and loss, and empowering others to create lives rooted in authenticity and joy.

You describe your coaching as "heart-centred" and strengths-based. How did you first arrive at that philosophy, and was there a pivotal moment or mentor who shaped it?

My introduction to strengths philosophy came the year I joined Gallup as a senior consultant in New Zealand. I had always had a very positive and optimistic approach to life, and finding strengths language to describe myself and others was both inspiring and illuminating.

My investment into heart-centred leadership, and promoting a more loving approach to life more generally came through the lived experience of losing my wife to brain cancer in 2021. She was an extraordinary person who was a real role model for me in living unconditional love. When she passed away, my love for her had to be expressed through other means, which led to the launch of Expansive.Love and my Let's Talk Love card deck which makes conversations about love more accessible for families and high trust teams.

In working with entrepreneurial couples, what is the most common tension you observe between partnership and business, and how do you help clients navigate it?

The most common tension tends to be the allocation of time, and time as a surrogate for love in many cases. What is the value of a profitable business built on 60 or 70 hours per week if the quality time with the most important people in your life suffer? Alongside this is the respect and celebration of each person's talents, what they do best, and what they love most in the business. My investment with clients is to help them clarify and articulate what is most important to them in life and business (values), and to identify how a couple will nurture a loving relationship both for each other and for their children where relevant. Ideally the business serves

---

Christopher Miller inspires with practical guidance, heartfelt wisdom, and transformative insights that encourage readers to live fully and lead with authenticity.

---

this outcome rather than the owners feeling burdened by the responsibility and aspiration of commercial success.

Your site mentions "building a practice you're proud of while living the life you've dreamed." What does "balance" mean to you personally, and how do you maintain it in your own life?

I have designed my life intentionally to prioritise my sons Cameron and Ross who are my absolute favourite and most important people. My self-employment gives me lots of flexibility to be present for them and actively participate in some of their activities, including the sport of springboard and platform diving. Often you can find me at the pool watching Ross train and writing my next book or communicating with clients via messaging.

Tell me about the process behind your book Finding FISH in a Strengths-Based Practice — what were your biggest challenges in writing it, and what surprised you in the course of researching or composing it?

I wanted the book to be full of practical examples, case studies and commentary from strengths experts other than myself. This meant quite a lot of very intentional research to align to each chapter of the book, and in the editing, integrating all of the examples with the core text of the manuscript. This was quite different to my first book (The Joy of

Finding FISH – a journey of fulfilment, inspiration, success, and happiness) which just kind of flowed out of me in a fairly sequential way, with many of my coaching philosophies and the journey of loving and losing Fiona downloading almost as a stream of consciousness. There was something more deliberate, structured and intentional about Finding FISH in a Strengths-Based Practice.

How do you integrate your coaching, writing, and mentoring work in a way that each feeds the other, rather than competing for your time or focus?

My writing occurs largely at weekends and I have a habit of taking the dog for a walk in an early morning, making a pot of coffee, and then sitting down for up to 4 hours generating a chapter or more. My coaching and mentoring takes place during the week and is scheduled in a way that enables me to do the school run and attend after school sports. My coaching / mentoring questions, relationship with my clients and impact stories often turn up in my writing, either anonymously or attributing to my clients when they are comfortable to be highlighted. None of my life feels like a competition as I love all of it and relish the variety of activity and relationships.

To give a sense of a typical week, Monday is generally sales, reach outs and social media planning. Tuesday morning is practice strategy and admin with my practice manager. Tuesday to Thursday is client sessions. Friday is strengths-based, heart-centred webinar (monthly) and recording for my Expansive-Love Dialogues podcast. Saturday morning is writing and the rest of the weekend is with family.

In your years of mentoring other coaches, what recurring blind spots or limiting beliefs do you most often see them wrestle with? And how do you help them move past them?

The biggest one that me and my clients continue to grapple with is a guilt-free approach to getting paid to do what you love. Most of my clients are living their dream AND have a sense of guilt that they do not deserve it, or that their work should feel like work rather than the joy it is. Feeling deeply grateful for what you have and your living/working experience is the precursor to helping others build the life of their dreams as well.

If you could go back and observe your author/self when you published your first major work, what advice would you give that earlier self?

My first book was a bit of a blur as I wrote a significant portion of it after Fiona was diagnosed with brain cancer, and wrote the last 5 chapters three months after she passed away. I was in a state of shock, and writing felt very therapeutic to sort through lots of emotions and to write the book as a tribute to her, and a moment in history for my boys to read sometime in the future. I don't think I'll ever write another book in quite the same way, though the emotion I am putting into the third FISH book (ExpansiveLove) is a little similar to the first. Fiona's legacy of unconditional love features heavily in book 3.

Which authors, thinkers, or coaches do you most frequently return to for inspiration or recalibration, and why do they speak to you?

Professionally, three of my greatest inspirations have been Sir John Whitmore (one of the founders of modern day coaching and author of Coaching for Performance), Tom Rath (prolific author both for Gallup and independently; Strengths-Based Leadership is genius for its perspective about both leadership and followership strengths profiles) and Jim Collins (famous for Good to Great, but all of his books offer highly detailed, evidence-based perspective on how to run an exceptional organisation; some of the case studies are now outdated but the principles remain very relevant).

For running a solo practice and practical advice to improve my own commercial success, I am grateful to Matt Church of the Thought Leaders Business School and author of The Thought Leaders Practice alongside Peter Cook and Scott Stein.

My most recent professional mentor is Lisa O'Neill who is an absolute inspiration and expert in Energy in every way.

Looking ahead, what themes, questions, or challenges do you think are emerging in the coaching / personal-development space that authors and practitioners should pay attention to?

I think the integration of artificial intelligence and the ability of coaches to leverage technology while remaining authentic and unique in the way they deliver their impact with clients is going to be fascinating to watch. Authors / coaches / thought leaders are experimenting with avatars that have the potential to keep intellectual property alive long after the original creator has died. What is not clear is how this remains commercial in an age of free, searchable content, and who owns it.

Finally, for authors who aspire to build a sustainable, meaningful writing or coaching practice, what are the key pieces of advice or guiding principles you would offer them (especially those just starting out)?

Don't worry about being perfect – I have a motto that suggests that in my own zone of genius, 80% is probably good enough. And everyone has a zone of genius – somewhere at the junction of what you do best, and what you love most. People buy your energy. If you are inspired and excited, someone else will be as well, and likely willing to pay you for it.

Be open to learning in order to hone your craft. I have recently completed my 5th coaching credential over the course of 18 years and I never tire of learning a new approach to a profession I deeply love.

I am pretty sure that everyone on the planet has a book in them, but not everyone has the courage to bring it into the light. Be brave, life is short.

"Britain's Greatness Lies In Its Blend"
An Interview With Solicitor Buket Erdoğan
Championing Equity, Innovation, and Britain's Strength in Diversity

Photo: *Buket Erdoğan: A Leading Voice in Immigration Law and Advocacy, Combining Expertise With a Passion for Innovation and Fairness*

"
We cannot make Britain great by closing ourselves off. We make it great by opening wisely, by being fair, and by remembering that our differences have always been the source of our greatest strength."

As the UK government moves forward with new immigration proposals — including plans to extend the qualifying period for Indefinite Leave to Remain from five to ten years — many are asking what this means for integration, fairness, and the nation's future. We spoke with Buket Erdoğan, a solicitor originally from Turkey and long-term Bristish resident, who offers a thoughtful and balanced perspective on immigration, belonging, and Britain's evolving identity.

By ELEANOR WILSON

Buket Erdoğan is a name that resonates with expertise, integrity, and forward-thinking in the fields of UK immigration and litigation law. Over the past decade, her remarkable work has helped countless individuals and businesses navigate some of the most complex legal landscapes while building futures in the United Kingdom. As a specialist in visa categories like family visas, human rights applications and appeals, settlement and naturalisation applications as well as skilled worker, global talent, and innovator founder visas, she not only supports clients with precision and care but also advocates for fair and sustainable immigration solutions. Erdoğan's commitment to her craft, her clients, and to the broader societal implications of her field sets her apart as a truly remarkable legal mind.

As the Solicitor of Immigration at Ashton Ross Law, Erdoğan combines her deep understanding of regulations with a passion for innovation, ensuring her clients benefit from the most up-to-date and pragmatic legal strategies. What makes her even more compelling is her dedication outside the courtroom—Buket is not just a solicitor but also a prolific writer, offering invaluable insights on the UK's evolving legal and technology landscape. Through her thoughtful commentary and thought-leadership articles, Erdoğan demystifies immigration processes while addressing broader societal and economic issues with clarity and depth.

At *Mosaic Digest*, we are thrilled to feature Buket Erdoğan in this issue, where her wisdom and refined perspective illuminate one of the most pressing global topics of our time: immigration and integration. Beyond her unparalleled expertise, Buket is a champion of Britain's strength through diversity—advocating for policies that are both equitable and forward-looking. Her articulate and compassionate voice underscores the importance of balancing progress with identity, and her approach is an inspiring reminder that legal frameworks can be tools for empowerment and inclusion.

In this insightful conversation, Erdoğan shares her views on proposed changes to UK immigration law, the challenges of integration, and the need for policies that reflect both the complexities of migration and the values of fairness and respect. As someone who embodies Britain's dynamic, multicultural identity, she reminds us that diversity is not just a fact of life here—it is a cornerstone of the nation's story.

Can you provide an overview of the government's proposed changes to immigration policy, including the extension of the indefinite timeline from five years to ten years? How will this affect migrants already living in the UK?

The proposal to extend the qualifying period for Indefinite Leave to Remain from five to ten years is one of the most significant reforms in years. The intention is to ensure that settlement reflects long-term contribution and commitment to the United Kingdom.

However, for those who have already built their lives here in good faith, such a change could be unsettling. People make decisions about homes, children and careers based on existing timelines. If the rules shift midway, it risks eroding trust. Transitional provisions must therefore protect those already on the five-year route. Policy should never penalise those who have done everything right.

It is also causing families chaos and extreme stress, most recently among Transport for London workers who are frontline staff, as well as many other visa holders who now face uncertainty about their future.

What challenges do migrants currently face due to the proposed policy changes, such as extending the indefinite leave timeframe? Do you foresee an impact on integration and stability?

Integration depends on security. When migrants spend a decade renewing visas and paying fees, uncertainty becomes their constant companion. Without a clear sense of permanence, it is harder to feel part of the community.

True integration happens when people feel stable and welcome enough to invest in their surroundings, to open businesses, to volunteer and to contribute to society. Extending the settlement timeline risks keeping people in a prolonged state of waiting, which undermines that process.

Buket Erdoğan is a trailblazing legal expert whose vision, compassion, and professionalism redefine immigration law and inspire systemic progress.

What safeguards, if any, exist to ensure that both legal migrants and asylum seekers aren't left in limbo for an extended period with the proposed extensions?

There must be both legal and practical safeguards. Transitional arrangements should protect those who entered under the five-year rule. Families and children must not face unnecessary delays that separate them or keep them in uncertainty.

Equally important is efficiency. Immigration backlogs can cause as much harm as policy changes. Timely, transparent decisions help people feel respected and allow them to move forward with dignity.

How do you think the current scale of immigration, with net migration at 430,000 in 2024, impacts the UK's infrastructure, public services and general societal harmony?

The number is significant, but migration is often blamed for issues that have deeper roots. The housing shortage, NHS pressures and strains on education stem from years of underinvestment and planning constraints. Migration interacts with these problems, but it did not create them.

In truth, migrants are vital to the very services under strain. They are doctors, nurses, teachers, engineers and carers. Many hold Skilled Worker,

Global Business Mobility, Global Talent or Innovator Founder visas. They pay taxes, contribute to National Insurance and often pay international tuition fees for their children. Migration brings challenges, but it also drives progress.

Polling suggests that a significant portion of the public considers immigration divisive and desires lower levels of migration. How can the UK government address public opinion while balancing the need for economic growth and migrant rights?

Public opinion must be heard, but leadership requires both empathy and evidence. The government should communicate clearly how migration benefits the economy and supports public services. If people see a process that is firm, fair and transparent, they are more likely to trust it.

Britain has always thrived as a nation that is both open and orderly. Protecting borders and recognising contribution are not opposites; they are two sides of a healthy national identity.

Prime Minister Sir Keir Starmer recently warned of the UK becoming an "island of strangers." How should policymakers constructively handle concerns about cultural change without fostering fear or prejudice?

Britain has never been an island of strangers; it has been an island of shared stories. Every chapter of our history has been shaped by people who came from elsewhere and found a home here.

We should also remember that Britain once carried its own vision, language and institutions to distant places such as Australia, New Zealand, Canada, India, parts of Africa and the Caribbean, building enduring bonds of law, trade and culture. If we were once able to extend that vision outward, surely we can now welcome those who arrive here safely and seek to contribute in return.

Migration, when managed responsibly, continues that same tradition of exchange. It strengthens our economy, enriches our culture and renews our sense of purpose. Cultural change should be met not with fear, but with curiosity and care. A confident nation does not see diversity as a threat; it sees it as a reflection of its own history and its greatest strength.

Immigration places a strain on public services such as housing, healthcare and education. For example, a home reportedly needs to be built in England every five minutes to meet demand. How realistic is it for the UK to adapt its infrastructure to keep up with migration levels?

The housing crisis is real, but migration is only one element of it. Underbuilding, planning restrictions and decades of underfunding are larger causes. Migrants are often part of the solution: builders, planners, architects and engineers who help expand capacity.

Britain can adapt, but it must invest wisely and modernise its systems. Blame will not build a single home; collaboration will.

Studies indicate non-EU immigration has the highest fiscal costs to the UK Treasury. In your opinion, how can policymakers develop a more economically sustainable immigration system?

We must look beyond first impressions. Skilled migrants and entrepreneurs contribute far more over time than early fiscal data might suggest. They create businesses, pay taxes and bring innovation.

The government's Global Talent Drive, backed by a £54 million fund, was launched to attract world-class researchers and innovators. It proves that the UK recognises talent from abroad as essential to its economic future. A sustainable system is one that values contribution, not origin.

How significant is the issue of illegal immigration, such as small boat crossings? What steps can be taken to reduce illegal arrivals while safeguarding human rights and international obligations?

Illegal migration is a serious concern, but it must be met with both firmness and fairness. Smuggling networks should be dismantled and asylum claims decided swiftly. Those without grounds should be returned, while genuine refugees, those fleeing necessity rather than opportunity, must be protected.

Safe, capped humanitarian routes are the humane alternative. Protecting borders and protecting people can and must coexist.

Do you believe the government's proposals adequately differentiate between migrants who can contribute positively to the economy and those seeking refuge from adverse situations? How should the UK approach this balance?

That distinction is vital. Economic migrants come to contribute through skills and enterprise; refugees come seeking safety and dignity. Both deserve respect, but they must be approached through different systems.

A new era in the United Kingdom's immigration system has begun with the introduction of HC 1333, a reform package that reshapes not only the routes to entry and stay but also the pathway to settlement. The consolidation of refusal grounds under the new Part Suitability signals a decisive shift toward a more uniform and stringent framework, applying equally to temporary and permanent routes. However, the proposed increase of the qualifying period for settlement from five to ten years, and its potential retrospective application to those already on their route to Indefinite Leave to Remain, has raised serious concern among migrants, employers, and legal practitioners. Such a measure would fundamentally alter the expectations of thousands who have lawfully built their lives in the UK, and it is widely believed that this aspect of the reform must be revisited with fairness and legal certainty at its core.

The UK should remain selective yet compassionate, attracting the skills that drive growth while honouring its humanitarian commitments. Whether someone has been here for five years or five hundred, the goal remains the same: to build, to belong and to contribute to the shared story of this country.

We cannot make Britain great by closing ourselves off. We make it great by opening wisely, by being fair, and by remembering that our differences have always been the source of our greatest strength.

The Brisley Bell: A picture-perfect Norfolk retreat with award-winning gardens, exquisite dining, and warm country charm

Outstanding Opulence At The Brisley Bell

Where Norfolk's Heritage Meets Modern Hospitality

The Brisley Bell is more than just an enchanting Norfolk pub—it's a celebration of community, heritage, and vision, brought to life under the extraordinary leadership of Amelia Nicholson. As co-owner, Amelia's remarkable journey through creative industries, from theatre to antiques, has shaped the soul of this award-winning inn in deeply meaningful ways. Mosaic Digest is thrilled to feature Amelia and her endeavours in this exclusive interview, where we explore the story behind The Brisley Bell's transformation into a boutique haven that seamlessly blends rustic charm with contemporary elegance.

Amelia's artistry and eye for detail are evident in every corner of the inn—from the thoughtful interiors that welcome guests with warmth to the carefully crafted pub gardens recognized as some of the finest in the UK. Her background in directing and producing adds a layer of ingenuity and storytelling that elevates The Bell far beyond its beautiful exterior, creating an experience that resonates long after the visit.

Joined in stewardship by Marcus Seaman, whose farming roots and entrepreneurial spirit bring a deep understanding of rural hospitality, and Chef Hervé Stouvenel, a culinary master with Michelin training, The Brisley Bell champions the best of Norfolk. Whether it's showcasing hyper-local ingredients, nurturing partnerships with regional producers, or creating spaces where history and modernity coexist in perfect harmony, Amelia and her team make an indelible mark on the inn's legacy and the surrounding community.

"We were determined that every space in our pub would be equally inviting."
– Amelia Nicholson

Amelia Nicholson and her team at The Brisley Bell transform a 17th-century inn Amelia's creativity, vision, and attention to detail make her a pioneer in blending artistry and hospitality at The Brisley Bell. Photos by Nathan Neeve

At Mosaic Digest, we celebrate creators who weave their passions into spaces that delight, inspire, and sustain—and Amelia Nicholson embodies that ethos beautifully. In this interview, she generously shares the journey, challenges, and vision behind The Brisley Bell, offering words of wisdom and glimpses into the heart that beats behind their success.

What inspired you both to take on the challenge of restoring a 17th-century inn into such a thriving destination?

Amelia Nicholson and her team at The Brisley Bell transform a 17th-century inn into a stunning destination blending hospitality, heritage, and heart.

We were both seeking a change in career and decided to pool our resources. In all honesty, we weren't looking to work in hospitality, we were looking for a challenge, a project, but it could have been in any industry. We both used to drink at the pub when we were younger - and lived locally - when it happened to come up for sale. It had been left derelict for four years, which was such a shame, and we really needed somewhere new to eat in the area as there was very little choice. Our business plan made sense… so we took the plunge. It was an amazing, creative time!

Could you tell us about the process of blending the inn's traditional rustic features with contemporary design elements?

In the 80's and 90's many pubs extended their restaurant space without much thought of how the new spaces connected to the old. The result was often lifeless rooms that lacked atmosphere. We were determined that every space in our pub would be equally inviting, so we took time to integrate old and new. It was also unaffordable to kit the pub out entirely in quality traditional wooden furniture and panelling, so we had to design our way out of this problem, which then inspired the modern elements.

The gardens are regarded as some of the finest pub gardens in the UK. What vision or ideas shaped their transformation?

Our vision was to design a space that invited guests to explore and relax, where every path or seating area offered something to discover. From the start, we imagined a shared space that encouraged people to slow down - a place to sit, linger, talk and feel at home. We didn't wish for it to resemble a commercial garden; rather, to evoke the charm of a garden belonging to a rural country home.

We wanted the garden to be as much of a draw as the pub itself - not just a backdrop, but a space guests would actively enjoy whilst being practical to the pubs needs. Being inland in Norfolk, we knew we needed to be unique to stand out and saw the potential to create a destination garden that felt just as layered, welcoming, and considered as our food and interiors.

A beautifully plated gourmet dish featuring a golden pastry filled with creamy topping, garnished with vibrant edible flowers and fresh greens, served on a rustic wooden table in an inviting dining setting.

How important is working with local farms and suppliers in crafting the restaurants seasonally led menu?

It's vital - both to support the local economy and to build trusted relationships while reducing our carbon footprint. It's far more rewarding to work with suppliers we can meet, visit, and collaborate with directly. A seasonally led menu just makes sense; Marcus comes from a farming family, Norfolk is a farming county with some of the best soil in the country, and we're surrounded by exceptional local produce.

We also forage ourselves - for samphire on the marshes or buckets of apples, cherries, pears, and even quail eggs gifted by locals with bumper crops. There's a lovely full-circle synergy when we serve guests dishes created by Hervé, using the produce they have shared with us.

The Brisley Bell combines boutique luxury with the relaxed feel of a pub. How do you strike the right balance between these two elements?

The hardest balance is managing guests' expectations, as the beauty of being a freehold, independent venue means our offering is like no other. Some guests may be expecting a reception desk or room service, and others delight in how spacious and quiet the rooms are for a pub. What we can guarantee is an authentic welcome. We're earthy and agricultural but we do everything with care, passion and attention to detail - and that's where the luxury comes in!

What makes Chef Hervé Stouvenel's approach to cuisine so unique, and how does his Michelin training influence the dining experience?

Hervé brings a calm precision and deep respect for ingredients that stems from his Michelin training. His cooking is refined but never fussy - he understands balance and lets flavours speak for themselves. He's equally comfortable preparing a classic French sauce

A stunning culinary display at The Brisley Bell featuring artfully plated dishes of locally sourced ingredients, showcasing refined flavours and rustic charm against a cozy and elegant backdrop.

as he is creating a British Sunday roast and his versatility keeps our menu exciting and grounded in both skill and seasonality.

Do you feel a responsibility to reflect and champion the heritage of The Brisley Bell and if so, how do you achieve this?

Absolutely! We're just custodians in a long line of landlords since 1706. We feel very strongly that pubs are a part of British culture that need to be nurtured. The British 'do' pubs brilliantly and that's something to celebrate, particularly in rural areas where they are often the hub of the community.

Since opening, we've taken part in and documented national celebrations, and we've researched and published the pub's history on our website (after earlier records were sadly lost in a fire). We keep contributing to that story - for instance, a local painting group led by Country Life cartoonist, Annie Tempest, spent a year painting locals, and their portraits now hang on our walls. We're also tagging over 30 trees we planted in the garden, recording their species and planting dates for future generations.

Amelia, does your experience as a theatre director influence the way you create an enjoyable and memorable experience for visitors?

I suppose it may. In theatre, the best productions often appear effortless, yet every detail has been carefully considered. A shared experience should resonate long after it's over, and that's true for hospitality too. It's all in the detail. Marcus and Hervé share that belief, and I think that's what makes us such a great team.

Marcus, how has your farming background shaped your outlook on running the inn and its restaurant in such a rural setting?

Farming teaches patience, practicality, and respect for the land, all qualities that translate directly to running a rural foodie pub. You learn to work with the seasons rather than against them, to value good produce. It's also a reminder that hard work and care over time yield real rewards - whether you're tending a field or running a business.

Unveiling A Visionary Of Chilling Fiction

EDDIE J. MORALES

Brings Horror To Life With Emotion, Innovation, And Imagination

BY MOSAIC DIGESTE STAFF

Eddie J. Morales, a remarkably talented author in the realm of modern horror fiction, has enthralled readers with his uniquely terrifying tales and emotionally complex narratives. A proud member of the Horror Writers Association (HWA), Eddie combines deep creative insight with professional expertise, blending elements of suspense, medical intrigue, and chilling visualizations that make his works feel like a cinematic experience. With five outstanding books to his name, Eddie's journey from crafting his first short story in high school to becoming a celebrated name in the horror genre is truly inspiring.

Through his imaginative ingenuity, Eddie has given life to unforgettable works like *Dreaded Tales: A Short Horror Story Collection* and *Zombie Mom*. His ability to merge heart and horror is striking, particularly in *Zombie Mom*, where the essence of maternal sacrifice is powerfully juxtaposed with zombie lore. Notably, Eddie's contribution to anthologies, such as *Phantom Menagerie*, elevated his profile within the community, earning buzz and admiration with "The Casket Bookcase," a dazzling story woven from the spine-chilling inspiration found during haunted tours.

In this exclusive feature, Mosaic Digest Magazine is honored to sit down with Eddie J. Morales to explore his creative processes, the personal connections behind his narratives, and the fascinating intersections between his education, experiences, and the horror genre. Join us as we celebrate the chilling brilliance of Eddie's imagination and his impactful contributions to contemporary horror literature.

Your passion for writing began in high school with "The House of Death," which later became part of Dreaded Tales. How did that early classroom success shape your confidence and trajectory as a genre writer?

When I received admiration from my classmates and English teacher for writing the story, the achievement sparked my interest in continuing with writing horror fiction. At that age, I already loved watching scary movies and television shows, which filled my imagination with creepy ideas. I later put the mindsets on paper and developed them into short horror stories. Thus, the early experience provided me with the inspiration I needed to continue my journey throughout the years, ultimately leading to the self-publishing of my books.

With a background in English Creative Writing and a Master of Health Administration, you blend creative and analytical thinking. How has your education influenced the themes and structure of your horror storytelling?

My education and experience in the healthcare profession have inspired my writing

> Eddie J. Morales discusses his passion for horror, blending emotional layers with suspense, his unique creative process, and how collaboration and real-world influences shape his genre-defining storytelling.

by blending what I learned in college and at work to develop my writing style of visualization. Readers often state that reading my stories is like watching a movie. In addition, many of my storylines incorporate pharmaceuticals and medical jargon, which create suspenseful scenes. Many can relate to such matters in their lives.

You're a member of both the Horror Writers Association (HWA) and the HWA Florida Chapter. What impact has been a part of these communities had on your work, growth, or advocacy within the horror genre?

Being a member of both groups has positively influenced my horror writing. Concerning HWA, the organization offers resources, such as guidance on protecting your work

and copyright information, which has helped me grow by understanding the business of writing and publishing. The HWA Florida Chapter is a fantastic group of individuals. The leaders do an excellent job coordinating monthly meetings. They keep members informed about current events while also offering meaningful writing workshops. It has helped me tremendously in building friendships with other writers with similar aspirations. I get to share my accomplishments and ask for support when needed in meeting my personal goals.

In Zombie Mom, you explore the deeply unconventional bond between a mother and her undead child. What inspired this emotionally layered twist on the zombie genre, and how did you balance horror with maternal instincts?

The concept of writing Zombie Mom came from a couple of circumstances. One was the loving relationship I had with my mother as a child. She would sacrifice to do anything necessary to take care of my two siblings and me. The other was my fascination with zombie movies, books, and TV shows. Both situations inspired me to write a story incorporating a mother's love for her baby, protecting him no matter what, even though he was born a zombie.

The story takes us from Georgia to Santa Fe, New Mexico, and includes elements of CDC and Homeland Security involvement. What research did you conduct to portray the institutional response to biothreats authentically in your narrative?

The research I conducted on the CDC and Homeland Security involved the types of training and responses that the government agencies provide in disaster preparedness. It includes precautionary measures involving individuals, such as isolation from the general public and monitoring their overall health. Though it may seem far-fetched that an actual zombie apocalypse emergency would happen, the current training offered to the staff of the agencies does help in dealing with other catastrophic events involving citizen casualties, including biological terrorist attacks.

Your short story "The Casket Bookcase" in Phantom Menagerie was on the recommended reading list, receiving Bram Stoker Award® buzz. How did this collaboration with other writers and the experience of writing-based inspiration tours influence your creative process?

It was an honor for my story to be placed on the recommended reading list on the Horror Writers Association website last year. It was the first time one of my stories was selected for an anthology, and collaborating with fellow talented writers was a pleasant experience. Each of us visited the haunted house, chose an item, and wrote a story based on the piece. The bookcase shaped like a casket caught my attention, inspiring me to write a scary story depicting where the item originated and how it made its journey to the house, leaving behind a body count. The creative process

Eddie J. Morales, acclaimed horror fiction author, shares his creative journey and insights into crafting unforgettable emotional and spine-chilling stories.

Eddie J. Morales masterfully crafts horror narratives that balance thrilling chills with emotional depth, solidifying his place as a genre innovator.

"

The early classroom experience provided me with the inspiration I needed to continue my journey throughout the years."

Eddie J. Morales

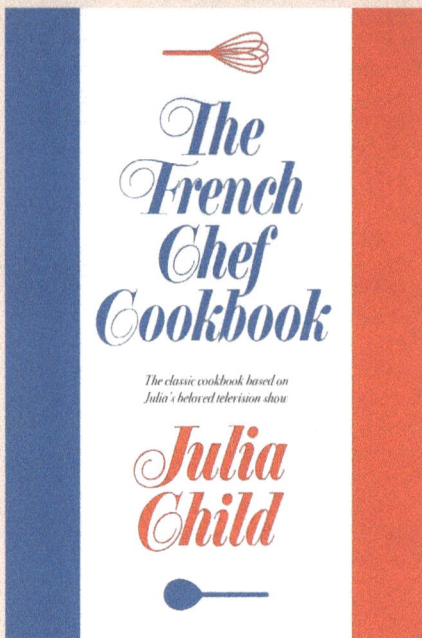

THE FRENCH CHEF COOKBOOK
by Julia Child

MELIZ'S KITCHEN
by Meliz Berg

THE NEW BASICS COOKBOOK
by Sheila Lukins

Julia Child's "The French Chef Cookbook" is a timeless culinary masterpiece, making French cuisine accessible, delightful, and inspiring for all.

The French Chef Cookbook by Julia Child is a timeless culinary classic that continues to inspire both novice and experienced cooks alike. This cookbook, which is a companion to her groundbreaking television series "The French Chef," encapsulates the essence of French cooking in a way that is accessible and engaging.

The book is meticulously organized, with each recipe presented in a clear and concise manner. Julia Child's unique voice and personality shine through in her detailed instructions and helpful tips. The recipes are accompanied by anecdotes and insights that make the cooking process enjoyable and educational.

The recipes in *The French Chef Cookbook* range from simple to complex, catering to a wide array of skill levels. Whether you're looking to master the art of making a perfect omelette or tackle the more challenging Coq au Vin, this cookbook provides the guidance needed to achieve culinary success. The step-by-step instructions are easy to follow, and the inclusion of ingredient substitutions and variations adds flexibility for home cooks.

The French Chef Cookbook is more than just a collection of recipes; it is a piece of culinary history. Julia Child's influence on American cooking is undeniable, and this book serves as a testament to her passion for food and education. It is a must-have for any cook interested in exploring the rich traditions of French cuisine.

The French Chef Cookbook by Julia Child is a valuable addition to any kitchen library. Its comprehensive and user-friendly approach makes it an essential resource for anyone looking to expand their culinary repertoire. Julia Child's legacy lives on through this cookbook, inspiring generations of cooks to embrace the joys of French cooking.

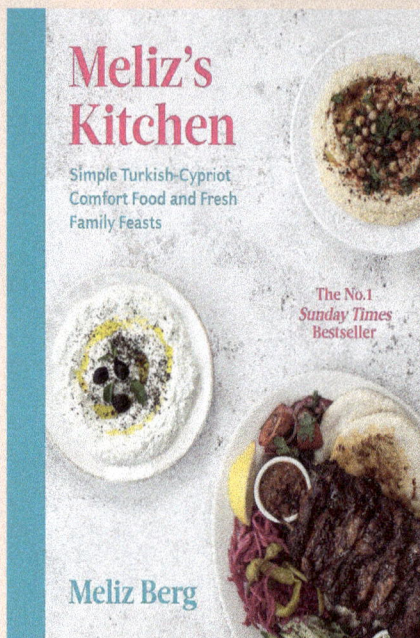

"Meliz's Kitchen" is a beautifully crafted cookbook, offering delicious, authentic Turkish-Cypriot recipes with easy-to-follow instructions and stunning photos.

Meliz's Kitchen by Meliz Berg is a delightful culinary journey into the heart of Turkish-Cypriot cuisine. This cookbook is a treasure trove of comforting and authentic recipes that bring the rich flavors and traditions of Turkish-Cypriot food right into your home kitchen.

One of the standout features of this book is its accessibility. The recipes are straightforward and easy to follow, making it perfect for both novice cooks and seasoned chefs looking to explore new culinary horizons. Meliz Berg's clear instructions and helpful tips ensure that even complex dishes are manageable.

The book is beautifully presented, with vibrant photographs that not only showcase the delicious dishes but also capture the essence of Turkish-Cypriot culture. Each recipe is accompanied by a personal anecdote or cultural insight, adding a warm and personal touch that makes the book feel like a conversation with a friend.

The variety of recipes is impressive, ranging from hearty mains to delectable desserts. Whether you're in the mood for a comforting bowl of Kıymalı Garavolli (minced lamb and pasta) or a sweet treat like Baklava, "Meliz's Kitchen" has something to satisfy every craving. The emphasis on fresh, wholesome ingredients ensures that the dishes are not only tasty but also nourishing.

What sets this cookbook apart is its ability to evoke nostalgia and create new memories. Many readers have shared how the recipes brought back fond memories of family meals and childhood flavors. It's a testament to Meliz Berg's skill in capturing the soul of Turkish-Cypriot cuisine and making it accessible to a global audience.

Meliz's Kitchen is a must-have for anyone interested in exploring the rich culinary traditions of Cyprus and Turkey. It's a beautifully crafted book that promises to bring warmth, flavor, and a touch of Mediterranean sunshine to your kitchen. Highly recommended!

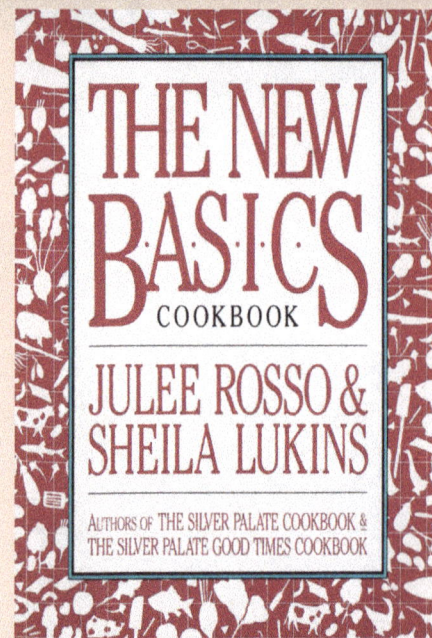

"The New Basics Cookbook" is a timeless treasure, offering diverse, delicious recipes with clear instructions and charming illustrations.

The New Basics Cookbook by Sheila Lukins and Julee Rosso is a comprehensive and beloved resource for home cooks. This cookbook, which follows the success of their "Silver Palate" series, offers a wide array of recipes that cater to both everyday meals and special occasions.

With over 875 recipes, this cookbook provides a vast selection of dishes, ensuring that there is something for everyone. From appetizers to desserts, the variety is impressive. The recipes are well-written with detailed instructions, making them accessible even for those who are new to cooking. The step-by-step guidance helps ensure successful results.

Throughout the book, the authors share valuable cooking tips and techniques that can enhance your culinary skills. These insights are particularly beneficial for those looking to improve their cooking. The book features delightful black and white illustrations that add a touch of charm and make it enjoyable to read. Many recipes include serving suggestions, which can help you create balanced and visually appealing meals.

However, some recipes can be quite complex and require a long list of ingredients, which might be overwhelming for beginners. There have also been reports of occasional errors in the recipes. Despite these minor drawbacks, *"The New Basics Cookbook"* remains a beloved classic that continues to inspire home cooks around the world.

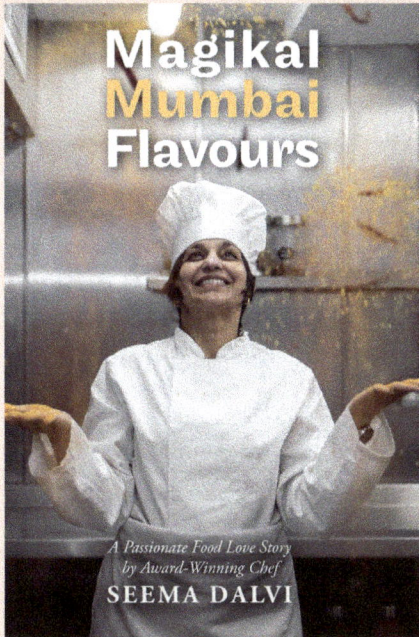

MAGIKAL MUMBAI FLAVOURS:
by Seema Dalvi

Magikal Mumbai Flavours is a captivating culinary journey, blending authentic recipes with rich cultural stories. A must-read for food lovers!

"*Magikal Mumbai Flavours: A Passionate Food Love Story*" by Chef Seema Dalvi is a delightful culinary journey that beautifully intertwines food and culture. This book is not just a collection of recipes; it is a heartfelt narrative that captures the essence of Mumbai's vibrant culinary scene.

The book is meticulously written and features stunning photographs that bring the recipes to life. Each page exudes a personal connection to the dishes, making it evident that Chef Seema Dalvi has poured her heart and soul into this work. The recipes are well-explained, making them accessible to both novice and experienced cooks.

One of the standout features of this book is the section that delves into the cultural significance of the recipes. Chef Seema provides insightful anecdotes and historical context, which enriches the reader's understanding and appreciation of Mumbai's diverse food heritage.

Readers have praised the book for its engaging storytelling and the authenticity of the recipes. The personal touch in the narrative makes it more than just a cookbook; it feels like a journey through Mumbai's bustling streets and aromatic kitchens. The book has received positive reviews for its ability to evoke nostalgia and inspire culinary creativity.

Magikal Mumbai Flavours is a must-have for anyone interested in Indian cuisine and culture. Chef Seema Dalvi has created a masterpiece that not only teaches you how to cook but also tells a passionate story of love for food and tradition. Whether you are a food enthusiast or someone looking to explore new culinary horizons, this book is a treasure trove of flavors and stories waiting to be discovered.

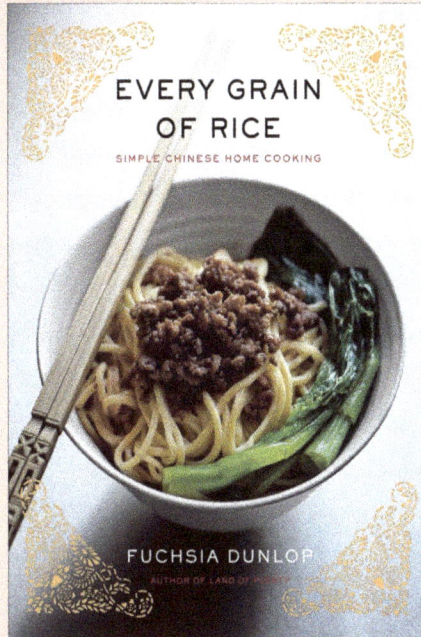

EVERY GRAIN OF RICE
by Fuchsia Dunlop

Every Grain of Rice by Fuchsia Dunlop is a culinary treasure, offering simple, authentic Chinese recipes with clear instructions and beautiful photos.

Every Grain of Rice: Simple Chinese Home Cooking by Fuchsia Dunlop is a culinary gem that brings the rich and diverse flavors of Chinese home cooking to your kitchen. As someone who loves exploring different cuisines, I found this book to be an invaluable resource.

The book is beautifully presented with clear, vibrant photographs that make each dish look incredibly appetizing. Dunlop's writing is engaging and informative, providing not just recipes but also insights into Chinese culinary traditions and techniques. This makes the book suitable for both beginners and experienced cooks.

One of the standout features of this cookbook is its focus on simplicity and authenticity. The recipes are straightforward and use ingredients that are relatively easy to find, even if you don't live near a specialty Asian market. This accessibility is a huge plus for home cooks who want to try their hand at Chinese cooking without feeling overwhelmed.

The variety of recipes is impressive, covering everything from hearty soups and stir-fries to delicate dumplings and refreshing salads. Each recipe is well-explained, with step-by-step instructions that are easy to follow. I particularly appreciated the tips on preparation and cooking techniques, which helped me achieve the best results.

Every Grain of Rice is a must-have for anyone interested in Chinese cuisine. It not only provides delicious recipes but also educates and inspires. Whether you're a novice cook or a seasoned chef, this book will undoubtedly become a cherished part of your culinary library.

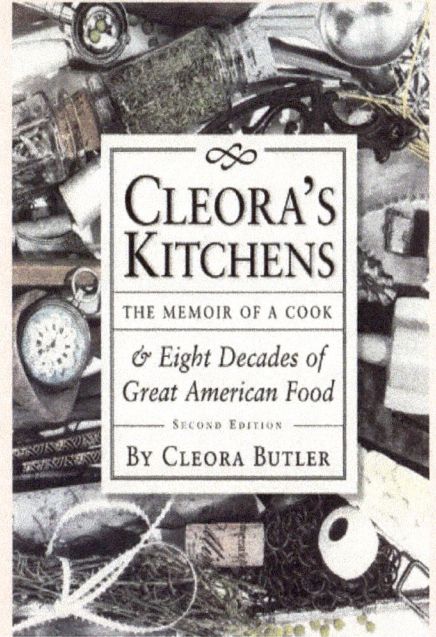

CLEORA'S KITCHENS
by Cleora Butler

Cleora's Kitchens" beautifully intertwines personal stories and recipes, celebrating African American culinary heritage with warmth and authenticity.

Cleora's Kitchens by Cleora Butler is a captivating blend of memoir and cookbook that offers a unique glimpse into the evolution of American cuisine through the eyes of an African American cook. Spanning eight decades, Butler's narrative begins with her childhood in Texas and follows her journey through various kitchens, capturing the essence of African American culinary traditions and their impact on American food culture.

The book features over 300 recipes, each a testament to Butler's rich culinary heritage and the diverse influences that shaped her cooking. From Southern classics to innovative dishes, the recipes are presented with detailed instructions and personal anecdotes that bring them to life. Butler's storytelling is engaging and heartfelt, providing readers with a deep sense of connection to her experiences and the historical context in which she lived.

Readers have praised "Cleora's Kitchens" for its authenticity and the warmth of Butler's narrative. The memoir is not just a collection of recipes but a journey through history, offering valuable insights into the cultural and social dynamics of the times. The book is enriched with historical tidbits, such as the origins of kitchen staples like graham crackers and food processors, adding an educational layer to the memoir.

Butler's stories are filled with nostalgia and emotion, making the book a compelling read. Her ability to weave personal experiences with culinary history offers a unique perspective on American food culture, particularly the contributions of African American cooks. "Cleora's Kitchens" is a must-read for culinary enthusiasts, history buffs, and anyone interested in the rich tapestry of American cuisine.

In summary, "Cleora's Kitchens" is a beautifully crafted memoir that celebrates the life and legacy of Cleora Butler. It is a valuable resource for preserving and honoring African American culinary traditions, making it a cherished addition to any kitchen library.

Unveiling A Visionary Of Chilling Fiction

JANNA YESHANOVA

Inspires Through Her Transformative Journey And The Power Of Love

BY MOSAIC DIGESTE STAFF

Janna Yeshanova embodies a spirit of resilience, creativity, and courage that shines through both her life story and her literary works. Born in the Soviet Union to a family of attorneys, Janna was raised in an environment steeped in literature and driven by ambition. Her remarkable journey—from escaping the crumbling Soviet Union with nothing but $126 to starting anew as an educator, conflict resolution expert, leadership trainer, and eventually an acclaimed author—speaks to the transformative power of persistence and hope.

Janna's novel *Love Is Never Past Tense* is not just a piece of fiction; it is a deeply personal tale inspired by her own real-life experiences of love, separation, and reunion. The story, which rekindles the emotional complexities of her reunion with a long-lost love, Sergey, years after their initial separation, has resonated widely with readers. The book tackles themes of rediscovery, resilience, and the enduring power of love in ways that continue to captivate audiences and invite reflection. It is no surprise that readers have described it as cinematic and deeply touching—a work that feels as alive as the author who penned it.

Through her writing, cultural transition from the Soviet Union to the United States, and professional reinvention as a life coach and speaker, Janna delivers powerful lessons on the importance of growth, adaptation, and standing firm in the face of cultural challenges. As the founder of LifeSpark LLC, she continues to guide others toward transformation, offering insights borne of her own extraordinary life.

We at *Mosaic Digest* are honored to feature Janna's inspiring story and to explore the life experiences that influence her poignant storytelling. Her work stands as a testament that even amidst uncertainty and adversity, one can thrive through love, courage, and truth. In reading her words, may our audience find as much hope as

her characters—and discover that sometimes, life truly does give second chances.

Your novel Love Is Never Past Tense is based on your real-life story of love, separation, and reunion. What inspired you to turn such a personal and emotional experience into a published novel, and how did the writing process help you reflect on that chapter of your life?

When national boundaries were drawn after World War II, a part of Moldova was split off to create Romania, creating an uncrossable border between two groups of my family. By 2008, I had been in America for nearly twenty years and decided to take a vacation to meet my Romanian cousins. As I was planning the trip, my old flame, Sergey, found me via the internet. He vowed he would die without me. I was hesitant, but the reunion was hard to resist. He drove from Moscow twenty-four hours nonstop to meet me. From there, we went to Odessa, Ukraine, where

> Janna Yeshanova shares her inspiring journey from the Soviet Union to the United States, her real-life love story, and how resilience and transformation shape her writing and coaching.

we had met decades earlier. The reunion inspired the book. The painful memories were overwhelmed by treasured reminders. I saw the same eyes, the same forehead with a dent, I heard the same voice. Who would not write a book after such?

Having grown up in the Soviet Union and then starting anew in the United States, how did your cultural transition shape your voice as a writer and your perspective as a storyteller?

I didn't write in the Soviet Union, except for some short stories, into a folder. Raising and developing a child took a lot of time. The way I think and express myself didn't change. I am very open, very sincere, and I speak my mind. The values are still the same.

I am saying what I think. Otherwise, I would feel uncomfortable. Yes, it was difficult to adjust

to a new culture. When I just started, I was Russian cultural consultant and Russian language teacher for several specialists at NCR who were working to penetrate the Russian market. During a lesson, one student put his feet on the table where we were all sitting--right in front of my face! Blood rushed into my head, but I made it to the end of the class. This job was the only income I had. The notion I got in the Soviet Union, all Americans put their feet on the table, prevailed over my desire to survive. At the end of the class, I told the students that I highly value their business, but I felt so insulted that my pride was shaken. Explaining why, I said that I would never come back. Later that evening, I heard the knock on the door. All of them were standing at the threshold. The guy who put his feet on the table came to apologize and asked me to come back. As the book will show, my cultural standards haven't changed, but American-Russian cultural disagreements were settled.

Your journey is rich not only in literary achievement but also in personal reinvention—as an educator, leadership coach, and speaker. How do these different roles influence your writing, especially when it comes to themes of resilience and transformation?

My book is packed with stories about overcoming obstacles to find opportunities. In that sense, the book became like a business card showing my resilience and the transformations I have been through.

In your career, both as an author and beyond, what would you consider the most defining or rewarding moment so far—one that truly affirmed your path?

I cannot select just one rewarding moment. Back in the USSR, I had a very interesting life of theatres, friends, gatherings, and lots of travel. I directed a play with my students that had huge success. My network included actors, scientists, artists, doctors, you name it. In America, as a life coach and speaker, I have talked to groups of hundreds of people.

There is a powerful scene in the book that takes place at the Vienna Railway Station. By standing up to bureaucracy, I helped over 300 hundred refugees whose lives were under threat. Even today, this is one of my proudest moments. I thought it was worth living just for this experience.

Many readers have found Love Is Never Past Tense deeply touching and cinematic. If it were adapted into a film, what key message or scene would you want the audience to carry with them most?

I would want them to carry with them a sense of hope—that in the midst of adversity, you can overcome if you never give up and continue to fight for whom you love and what you believe.

You've spoken about the importance of love, courage, and rediscovery. What advice would you give to aspiring writers who want to tell stories rooted in truth but fear vulnerability or exposure?

Many are afraid to share their experiences. They are afraid to be accused and ridiculed. My advice is going to sound cold: tell your story, tell it your way, or aspire to something else instead of writing.

Not ready to quit? Good for you! Look at your purpose, your motive, your why. Look for your audience—who is waiting for you to speak up? Compare potential benefits to risks. What are the likely outcomes? If the answer is nobody will read your work, then the outcome would be the same if you never sat down to write.

When did you first feel the book would be accepted?

On a plane trip, I decided to review galley proofs of the book. A gentleman in the next seat asked what I was doing and if he could see the book for a moment. I gave him the book, and he started reading it. He didn't talk to me again until we landed. He gave me the book, together with his business card. Please let me know when the book will be out there. I want to buy it. Oh! No! No! Don't buy it! I'll send it to you. I was so happy that someone was so interested in it. After I sent him the book, a couple of months later, his community in Omaha invited me to make a huge presentation.

Eddie J. Morales, acclaimed horror fiction author, shares his creative journey and insights into crafting unforgettable emotional and spine-chilling stories.

"

I am very open, very sincere, and I speak my mind."

Janna Yeshanova

Janna Yeshanova is a visionary storyteller who masterfully combines emotional depth, life lessons, and hope in her powerful novels.

Exploring Life, Literature, And Resilience

RAY ANYASI

Inspires Readers With Spellbinding Stories That Transcend Genres and Formats

BY MOSAIC DIGESTE STAFF

Ray Anyasi is a literary force whose works have deeply enriched Africa's literary landscape, leaving an indelible mark on readers across the globe. As one of Africa's most published authors, with over 25 titles spanning genres as diverse as fantasy, thrillers, poetry, and comics, Anyasi is a master storyteller who dares to traverse boundaries, creating unforgettable worlds that resonate universally. From the enthralling political crime thriller *A Poll of Vampires*, to the sweeping mythic realm of *Sorrows of Udi*, his ability to weave extraordinary tales of ordinary people confronting unimaginable challenges is both timely and timeless. Anyasi's books, translated into languages like Spanish, Portuguese, and German, not only capture the essence of the human spirit but have also achieved multimedia acclaim, with adaptations into comics and award-winning animated web series earning international recognition.

At Mosaic Digest magazine, where celebrating innovative voices is part of our mission, we are thrilled to feature this interview with Ray Anyasi, a writer whose craft goes beyond storytelling to illuminate cultural truths, universal struggles, and the power of resilience. From his pivotal work nurturing the next generation of African writers through Bookhouse Nigeria, mentoring programs, and #theWriteClubwithRayAnyasi, to his dynamic roles as Editor-in-Chief of Geek Digest and Festival Director at Rayany Creators Film Festival, Anyasi exemplifies what it means to be a writer who uplifts others while shaping his own magnificent literary legacy.

Join us as we delve into the world of Ray Anyasi—his journey, creative philosophies, and the stories that continue to inspire millions. Through this engaging interview, discover why Mosaic Digest proudly celebrates him as one of the finest voices in literature today.

You debuted fresh out of university with the political crime thriller A Poll of Vampires, and today you're celebrated for the epic fantasy series Sorrows of Udi. Can you walk us through the evolution of your storytelling—from your early foray into thrillers to the richly mythic worlds you now build in fantasy?

My storytelling journey has been quite interesting in that when I started out, I was something of an outsider in the world of writing. I didn't know much rules or what is considered the norm. I did know writers were for some reason supposed to stick to a genre. Because all my life, I read across many genres, when I started writing, I just wrote in any genre I felt my story is best suited.

Ray Anyasi shares his journey as one of Africa's most published authors, his creative philosophies, his impactful mentorship, and how he transforms extraordinary struggles into timeless, genre-defying stories.

You've said your writing is influenced by "extraordinary stories of ordinary people who must confront monstrous challenges." Could you share a specific real-life story—or memory—that first inspired you to write in this mode, and how it shaped your literary voice?

This largely comes from my early childhood and upbringing. My parents, intentionally or not, didn't try to shield us from the realities of our circumstances such that from a young age, I had a front row sit to life more than one would expect. When I was six or seven, we woke up one morning to a letter from the landlord saying the house we lived in has been sold and the new owner wants all tenants out in two weeks or be forceful-

ly evicted. So, there we were, facing a real possibility of homelessness. A year later or so, life was going smoothly for us, there's a national election coming which gave Nigerian so much hope for the future. Then the election was annulled in the most dramatic fashion, protests erupted in the city we lived, my parents who were self-employed at that time couldn't go to work and couldn't earn. Suddenly, we're living with penury. These thread of events that we didn't cause, didn't foresee but must confront to get through the day became part of the struggles of our existence. I wasn't surprised when I started writing and noticed it was a common theme in my stories.

Sorrows of Udi has been translated into multiple languages and even adapted into an animated web series that earned selections at international film festivals. What was it like to see your story come alive in that medium—and how did it reshape your understanding of storytelling across formats?

It was a surreal experience to see Sorrows of Udi in that first animated short. It gave me a whole new view of what that fictional world could become. As I see more and more of my stories transcend formats, I realize that prose, comics, film and drama might be starkly distinct formats with their own unique rules, but storytelling whatever the genre or format has one simple rule. To make the reader or viewer see themselves in the experiences of your characters. No matter how bizarre and outrageous character's experience is, if the reader can make a realistic connection of how a regular person's life can go that way, then the story slaps.

As founder of Bookhouse Nigeria, director at Naphtali Publishers, and creator of initiatives like #theWriteClubwithRayAnyasi and your mentoring programs, you're deeply committed to literacy and nurturing writing talent. What's been the most memorable moment—from a works-

hop or from a mentee—that reaffirmed your belief in investing in the next generation of African writers?

Back in 2018 when I was MD of Naphtali Books, I discovered a brilliant writer in Albrin Junior when we picked up his debut novel, Naked Coin. The amazing progress he's made in his journey as a storyteller today gives me so much joy and makes me want to keep doing what I do.

Broken Cloud: The First Sunrise is one of your most popular works. It's a fantasy world steeped in darkness and secret romance. What emotional or thematic core were you hoping to explore through Prince Ikan's struggle and Sarie's fate in a kingdom without sunlight?

My hometown has a saying that translates into, "The governor of a prison is also in prison." In Broken Cloud, the Ottas may have may have established a slavery system the benefits them but to keep the Otts enslaved, the slave masters must commit to activities that enforces and sustains slavery, thereby making the slave master a slave to the system of slavery.

You've written across genres—from political thrillers like Ujasiri and How to Terrorize Terrorism to poetry collections such as Lines of Thoughts and epic fantasies. How do you decide which medium or form best suits what you want to say—and how do faith and social commentary weave through these genres for you?

For me, it's all about which style, medium or genre does deserved justice to the characters whose stories I'm telling. I find that I tell a story in comics format when I'm keener about getting it done fast so it can be out of my head. I write poetry when a story carries too much emotional weight than prose can help. I write prose when a character's journey isn't straightforward and demands a rich emphasis of the plot to make it make sense to the reader.

Author Ray Anyasi, Africa's literary powerhouse, crafting stories that resonate globally and reimagine humanity's resilience and triumphs over adversity.

"

"The governor of a prison is also in prison—systems of power can enslave everyone connected to them."

Ray Anyasi

Jay Allan Storey Takes Readers On A Journey Through Genres, Adventure, And The Limits Of Imagination

By MOSAIC DIGEST STAFF

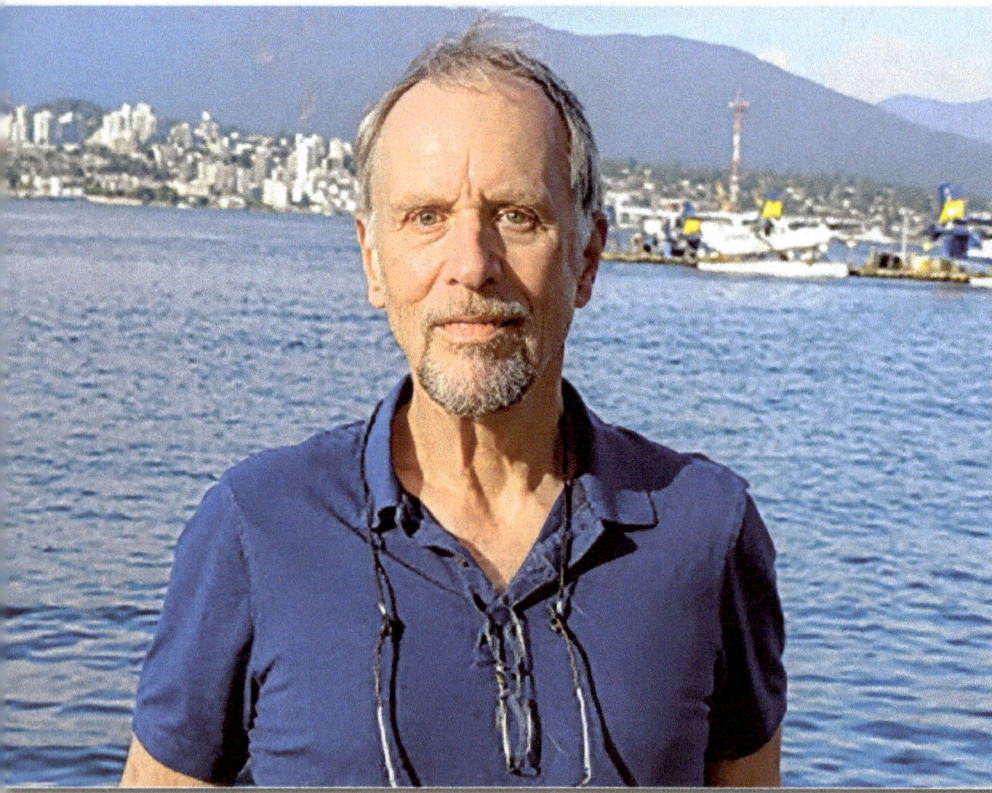

Photo: *Jay Allan Storey: A storyteller who bridges imagination and reality, crafting tales from dystopian futures to quirky mysteries. His work reflects a life of curiosity and adventure, inviting readers to dream and explore.*

Exploring Creativity, Global Travels, And Stories That Transform

Jay Allan Storey shares his creative process, global inspirations, love for music, and how his diverse life experiences shaped thrilling science fiction, mysteries, and genre-defying literary masterpieces.

Jay Allan Storey isn't just an author—he's a multi-dimensional creative force whose work transcends the boundaries of genre and imagination. From science fiction epics to meticulously crafted mysteries, Jay captures the complexity of human experience with stories that toe the line between the conceivable and the fantastical, always rooted deeply in the characters who bring them to life. He is as fearless in his writing as he has been in his remarkable life, traveling through the rugged terrains of Iraq, Afghanistan, and Pakistan, or exploring the more personal landscapes of music and creativity. Mosaic Digest is thrilled to feature this exclusive interview with an author whose diverse experiences and boundless curiosity have irreversibly shaped the dynamism of contemporary fiction.

Jay's bibliography reads like a treasure trove of literary innovation. Whether it's the daring thrillers like *The Arx, the immersive worlds of the Black Heart* and *Vita Aeterna* series, or the unpretentious charm of his latest mystery *The Houseboat Detective*, his work pushes genre expectations and invites readers into a thoughtful exploration of identity, transformation, and possibility. Take, for example, *The Houseboat Detective*, a departure from his hallmark science fiction into the world of mysteries, humor, and Canadian-centric narratives that celebrate the city of Victoria—Jay's birthplace and lifelong muse. His protagonists are more than characters; they are reflections of resilience and evolution, illustrating his belief that breaking free from stereotypes is not just possible, it's essential.

Through this editorial feature, Mosaic Digest celebrates Jay Allan Storey not just for his extraordinary stories, but for the richness with which he infuses his art—the music that harmonizes his narratives, the diverse experiences that lend authenticity to his work, and the global perspective that enriches his writing with layers of depth. His stories remind us that imagination doesn't have limits, and his journey proves that creativity flourishes best in lives lived boldly. Jay Allan Storey stands as an artist who invites us to not only dream about alternate realities but to embrace them as mirrors of our own. Immerse yourself in this interview, and prepare to be both inspired and intrigued by the mind of a literary craftsman at the peak of his creative brilliance.

Your career has spanned everything from software development to cab driving—how have these diverse experiences influenced your storytelling?

Though I didn't actually begin writing until quite late in life, I'd always considered the idea, and beyond just enjoying diversity, I've always been attracted to experiences that might provide future material. Many of the things I've done have made it into my books, and having actually done them I can talk about them with some kind of authority. Also, I think diversity of experience leads to diversity in thought, and opens the mind to new ideas.

What inspired you to shift genres with The Houseboat Detective, and how did writing a mystery differ from your usual science fiction work?

One of my earlier novels, The Arx, was a detective story, though it had a significant SciFi component, and I've always loved a

---

Jay Allan Storey is a bold storyteller who transforms innovation and life experience into unforgettable worlds and compelling narratives.

---

good mystery. Still, The Houseboat Detective is a departure from my usual work: it's the first time I've tried to incorporate humour, the first time there's been no science fiction involved, and the first time I've made a point of featuring locations from a particular city-Victoria, British Columbia.

The book is also more character driven than my other books, which have all featured 'big' ideas-Houseboat Detective is really just a pure mystery.

I've always resisted being stuck in a particular genre, and I like to challenge myself. Though I love science fiction, I wanted to try something different. Also, given the political turmoil currently surrounding Canada, I wanted to write something that was unabashedly Canadian-that featured the city where I was born and grew up. If Houseboat Detective proves to be popular, I'm hoping to make it a continuing series.

In keeping with the diversity and Canadian themes, I'm currently working on a new novel, which will be in the steampunk genre, and set in northern Canada.

You've travelled extensively through places like Afghanistan, Iraq, and the Swat Valley—how have those journeys shaped the themes or characters in your books?

I traveled around the world solo when I was nineteen, and that experience alone provided enough ideas to last a lifetime. There was a scene in my first book, Eldorado, where masses of people are living on the street, that was inspired by one of my experiences traveling in India.

I'm actually surprised that more of my travel experiences haven't made it into my books, at least explicitly, and that I've never been particularly inclined to write about those places, though they made a powerful impression on me. While they haven't had much explicit coverage, I'm sure they're implicitly there in the multifaceted way I view the wor-

ld, and the characters I portray.

Music seems to play a role in your creative process, especially in The Houseboat Detective. How do you use music to develop your characters or scenes?

I actually hadn't thought of it before, but in both my detective novels, The Arx and Houseboat Detective, the protagonists are musicians (though much more so in the Houseboat Detective). Maybe I somehow subconsciously relate the complexity of music to the complexity of an investigation.

In Houseboat Detective, music is what keeps the protagonist, Jake Sommers, going-'the one unmoving anchor in a life that, in every other way, seemed to drift aimlessly'. It uplifts him when he's down, and soothes him when he's stressed. It also informs his detective work. At one point he thinks-'Like a discordant note in an arpeggio, something stood out from everything else'.

Your novels are described as "skirting the edge of believability"—how do you strike the balance between the imaginative and the credible?

As primarily a science fiction writer, I'm aware that my audience are likely to be knowledgeable about science and in tune with what's scientifically feasible. They're always ready to 'pounce' if you make a glaring logical or technological error.

At the same time, I'm attracted to scenarios some might consider far-fetched, such as in The Black Heart of the Station, where the Earth is dragged out of its orbit by a passing perturbation of Dark Matter, or Vita Aeterna, where a treatment has been invented that can significantly extend human lifespan.

I think the balance between visionary thinking and believability is a problem every science fiction writer has to deal with. You want to use your imagination to visualize some outrageous alternate reality, but that reality still has to follow the basic rules of physics and biology.

Looking back at The Black Heart of the Station and Arrival, what do you consider the biggest creative breakthrough or lesson you gained from writing those books?

I've always been fascinated by the idea that biblical scriptures might refer to actual historical events-that the great flood, the parting of the Red sea, etc. might have been real occurrences whose details were lost in time. I wanted to write a story that would capture how such a circumstance might occur.

This is the premise driving the Black Heart. The action takes place in a self-contained city, the Station, built 1500 years in the past, 1 kilometer beneath the surface of a dead, frozen Earth. Around year 900, a catastrophic asteroid strike destroyed a huge section of the city, killing the vast majority of its inhabitants, and erasing virtually all historical data. The survivors, predominantly blue-collar workers with little knowledge of the technical and historical aspects of the Station, spent

the next hundred years barely hanging on. During those dark days, all knowledge of the past and the city's original purpose was lost, surviving only as mysterious parables in the texts of the resident Solis church.

Until the discovery of a hidden scripture by a novice Solis monk finally reveals the truth.

Diversity of experience leads to diversity in thought, and opens the mind to new ideas."

Jay Allan

Tim Bowler Inspires Readers And Writers Through A Brilliant Career And A Global Mentoring Journey

By MOSAIC DIGEST STAFF

Photo: *Tim Bowler, award-winning author of River Boy and mentor to writers worldwide, photographed during his creative mentoring session.*

Award-Winning Novelist Reflects On His Literary Journey

Tim Bowler discusses his celebrated writing career, global mentoring of authors, inspiration for River Boy, creative challenges, cultural storytelling influences, and the joy of empowering aspiring writers worldwide.

Tim Bowler, the extraordinary voice behind some of the most evocative and gripping works in British teenage fiction, has cemented his place as one of the finest authors of our time. With over twenty books to his name and sixteen literary awards, including the prestigious Carnegie Medal for *River Boy,* Tim's work transcends genres, introducing readers to powerful storytelling that resonates with emotional depth and psychological intrigue. His ability to blend mystery, philosophy, and humanity earned him accolades such as "the master of the psychological thriller," and his books continue to connect with audiences worldwide, having been translated into over thirty languages and selling over a million copies.

Here at *Mosaic Digest,* Tim Bowler's work holds a special place in the realm of storytelling excellence, inspiring readers and writers alike to delve into the unknown and uncover truths about themselves and the world around them. His novels— such as *Starseeker, Dragon's Rock,* and *Frozen Fire*—showcase an unwavering commitment to asking deep, existential questions while crafting plots that keep readers captivated. Beyond his own writing, Tim's mentorship of authors from across the globe—spanning generations and cultures—further reflects his devotion to empowering others to find their creative voices and tell their stories.

In this interview, we delve into Tim's unparalleled literary journey, his reflections on life-changing milestones, and the rewarding shift from author to mentor. His remarkable ability to inspire audiences as both a storyteller and a guide shines through every word, leaving us in awe not just of his boundless imagination, but also his profound kindness and humility. At *Mosaic Digest*, celebrating creative ingenuity is central to our mission, and Tim Bowler epitomizes the enduring power of art to touch lives, transcend boundaries, and spark the imagination

You've had an extraordinary writing career, with more than 20 books to your name, including the award-winning River Boy. Looking back, is there a moment or book that stands out as the most defining point in your career—and why?

River Boy winning the Carnegie Medal in 1998 was certainly a pivotal moment. It was my third novel and although my first two books, Midget and Dragon's Rock, had been well received, I wasn't sure that a mystical story about a young girl trying to cope with the oncoming death of her grandfather would garner much enthusiasm from readers, booksellers or critics. It was nice to be proved wrong! Sales of River Boy went through the roof and it went on to become one of my most popular titles, both in the UK and abroad. It also refocused reader attention on my earlier books and those that were to follow. But the Carnegie Medal win was defining in another sense too: it gave me a shot of self-confidence; and that, as most writers will tell you, riddled as we often are with self-doubts, is a rare and precious thing.

After turning 70, you chose to dedicate your time to mentoring aspiring writers around the world—ranging from children as young as six to adults in their eighties. What inspired this transition?

I was in my twenties and pushing to finish my first novel. I had to fit this around the various jobs I took on to earn a living, so I'd get

---

Tim Bowler is a literary luminary whose compelling novels and mentorship efforts inspire countless readers and writers worldwide.

---

up at three in the morning, grit away at the novel for a few hours, then go out to work. I was struggling with the writing, however, and felt I needed some guidance. A friend mentioned a retired writer in his late sixties who offered tutorials to aspiring authors. These were pre-internet days so writers would post him their extract, he'd speak his suggestions into an old-fashioned audio cassette, and send it back in a jiffy bag. I found it incredibly useful and although I didn't work with him for long, I decided that if I ever got anywhere in writing, I'd offer to help others in like manner when I reached a similar age – so here I am.

You now tutor writers from across the globe via Zoom, making your work more varied than ever. How has connecting with such a wide range of voices and cultures influenced your perspective on storytelling?

It has broadened it enormously. I have always enjoyed reading literature from around the world, usually in translation, but working directly with storytellers from other countries and cultures has been liberating for me. Every author, including those from very similar backgrounds, has his or her unique writing voice, and twenty such authors given an identical writing prompt will usually produce twenty utterly different stories. But factor in cultural, ethnic, spiritual and national differences as well and the stories become even more richly varied. Authors from China, Russia, Kuwait or wherever will make references to concepts that are entirely new to me. I marvel not only at this but at the fact that many of these authors are writing out of their mother tongue into near-perfect English. I don't think they have any idea just how much I learn from the experience of mentoring them or how much they inspire me.

When mentoring younger writers, particularly those of school age, what recurring strengths—or

challenges—do you notice? And how do you guide them while preserving their unique voice?

Tutoring young writers is a joy. They're embarking on a creative arc which I hope will burn brightly for the rest of their lives and I'm in the privileged position of being asked to help them. But the truth is, they don't need much help. They just need to be unleashed. They're creatively fearless. They're like small gods who haven't yet realised they possess superpowers. That's where I come in: showing them how good they are, how great they can be. It's a different dynamic teaching children, especially the very young ones. With adults I'm just me but to the kids (their parents tell me) I'm like a cross between an elderly sage and a handy extra grandfather. Whatever I am to them, however, to me they're all miracles, and whether they're writing about unicorns or saving the rainforest, they fill me with hope for the future of our world.

As someone who's spent decades writing fiction and is now deeply involved in editorial coaching, do you find that helping others refine their work has reshaped how you think about your own writing?

Yes, it has. I love editing manuscripts, not to impose my opinions on another author's work, God forbid, but simply to suggest improvements. Proofreading on its own would frustrate me. I would find it hard to correct all the mistakes in a text but not be empowered to recommend stylistic improvements. There is indeed a coaching aspect to this, as you rightly mention, and that's why I offer authors a joint copy and line edit. That covers the correction of mistakes but also allows my pedagogic side to express itself and hopefully help the author to look at the way he or she is using language. I also offer general manuscript critiques and both these editorial processes impact my own writing. By analysing so closely the writings of others, seeing what works and what doesn't, suggesting changes, pondering solutions, I realise that in a subtle way I'm coaching myself too.

With such a rich body of work and now this deeply fulfilling mentoring journey, what do you hope your literary and creative legacy will be—for both your readers and the writers you've helped along the way?

I never think about a legacy. I prefer to focus on being useful now. My aim, if this doesn't sound pretentious, is just to give good service. For me, that involves connecting with people and sharing a (hopefully wholesome) portion of myself with them. My books were one way in which I did that and I still receive lovely emails from readers, so that makes me feel I haven't written in vain. Mentoring and editing are other ways to connect and share and give something of myself. I wasn't sure anybody would be interested when I first offered my services two years ago but within six months I was crammed and now I've never been busier, or more professionally fulfilled. So I'm not sure about

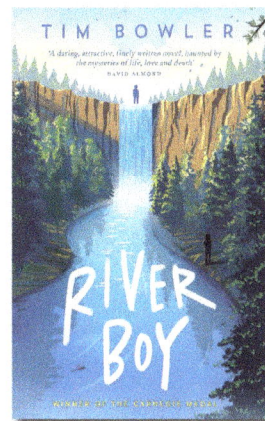

River Boy by Tim Bowler is a tender, poetic tale about life, loss, and acceptance. Jess's journey captures the bond between a granddaughter and her dying grandfather, blending realism with mysticism. Bowler's metaphorical river showcases life's flow beautifully. A gripping read that's emotional, artistic, and deeply inspiring. Suitable for all ages.

a legacy, but if anything I have ever written, said or done has left a warmth in someone's heart, I'll settle for that.

"

River Boy winning the Carnegie Medal in 1998 was certainly a pivotal moment."

Tim Bowler

A.W. Daniels

A.W. Daniels, acclaimed author of the Genetically Privileged series, reveals his creative process, explores issues of genetic ethics, and discusses the evolution of his characters in an engaging Mosaic Digest interview.

Leads Science Fiction Into Ethical Frontiers

Exploring Genetic Engineering, Ethics And Thrilling Characters

A.W. Daniels is a captivating storyteller whose imaginative mind charts paths into the uncharted realms of science fiction, blending humanity's greatest ambitions with the ethical quandaries of genetic engineering. Daniels' books—including the acclaimed *Genetically Privileged* series—challenge readers not only to embrace complex, futuristic worlds but also to reflect on the societal implications of tampering with the very fabric of human identity. A finalist in *50 Great Writers You Should Be Reading*, Daniels has an undeniable gift for weaving narratives that are as thought-provoking as they are entertaining.

In this exclusive Mosaic Digest interview, the author provides an intimate glimpse into his creative journey—from his early days pursuing a degree in biology, through a surprising detour into sales, to the powerful inspiration that awakened his talents as a writer. With a flair for crafting intricate characters and thrilling plots, Daniels expertly navigates themes of morality, ambition, and the unpredictable consequences of scientific advancement.

Readers of Mosaic Digest can count themselves fortunate for the opportunity to delve deeper into the mind of A.W. Daniels, whose work not only pushes the boundaries of storytelling but also pushes us to ponder the limits of our own humanity. Through layered narratives and ethically charged dilemmas, Daniels proves that science fiction is more than escapism; it's a lens through which we can glimpse possible futures and reckon with the choices we face today. We're honored to celebrate his creativity and intellect in a genre where big questions meet ingenious answers.

What inspired your transition from a background in biology and sales to writing science fiction thrillers like Genetically Privileged?

Writing has always been a personal release for me. The confining structure of business allows only for a limited amount of elaboration whereas writing fiction opens the mind to new ideas and situations. Though I do try to make my works plausible to the reader.

Your novels tackle complex themes around genetic engineering and societal ethics—what drew you to explore these futuristic and controversial topics?

Can you share your creative process—from the initial spark of an idea to completing a full-length novel?

These two questions have similar answers.

It was in Canada on a sales trip when my writing paramour reared her lovely head. I was reading an article about genetics and how the day of "designer babies" was soon coming to fruition. Was it the science or the writing aspect of the article that planted this seed of script in my thoughts?

How would society accept, or use, these children of manufactured superiority? Will the children allow outside influences to ultimately determine their roles and fate? So many questions on which to contemplate.

A year went by as a story took root. The social aspect of a genetically modified child continued to grow. What abilities could be scientifically born into a human? What would society think of such an engineered being? What would the children think of a society that was populated by humans inferior to his or herself? I found myself sitting at my laptop for hours on end as the story, already developed in my head, spewed onto the pages. The first draft was rough, very rough, but I stood up and felt the composition exhilaration from decades past.

What did being selected as a finalist for 50 Great Writers You Should Be Reading mean to you personally and professionally?

Recognition for one's work is a definite adrenaline rush. Seeing that others would view my writing in a positive light is unexplainably satisfying. Professionally, I have been with hope that it could be noticed in a similar light. Not having contacts in the publishing world has kept me from really polishing the works to a level needed in today's publishing forum.

Are you currently working on new stories within the Genetically Privileged universe, or exploring entirely new worlds and themes in your upcoming projects?

These two questions also have similar answers.

Character development is relatively simple for me since the works can grow with the characters natural, though accelerated, growth process. Privilegedook, Genetically Privileged, depicts the main characters as children. The second, Genetically Conflicted, depicts the main characters as teenagers.

I have a third in the works currently titled as Genetically Rejected which will depict the main characters as adults. The fourth and final untitled work will show the main characters as taking over. It will have an almost Mary Shelley – Frankenstein correlation though with a somewhat different outcome for the "monster".

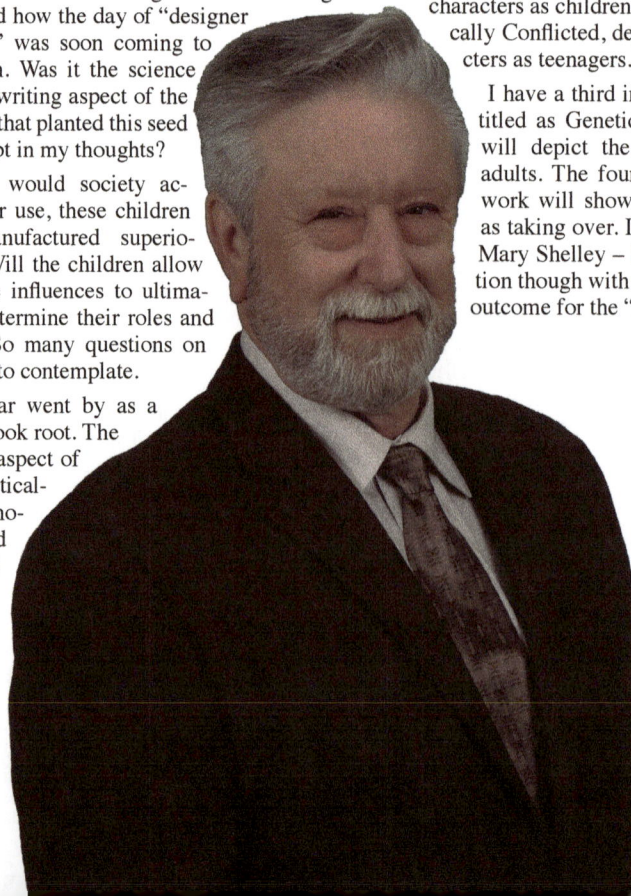

Ken Mooney

Ken Mooney is a dynamic author whose storytelling spans genres, blending mythology, horror, memoir, and LGBTQ+ romance with rare insight and emotional depth. Hailing from Dublin, Ireland, Ken's works, including *The Last Olympiad, The Astrocytoma Diaries,* and *Apocalypse… Whenever,* showcase his ability to craft compelling narratives that balance fantastical worlds with deeply human experiences. From exploring Greek gods in a modern, dark fantasy setting to courageously recounting his battle with a brain tumor, Ken's stories resonate with themes of grief, identity, chosen family, and resilience.

With a sharp intellect and a fearless creative approach, Ken stands out as a writer unafraid to tackle challenging truths while offering readers hope, reflection, and thrilling escapism. Mosaic Digest magazine proudly spotlights his creative journey, celebrating the rich legacy of an author who continues to redefine genre storytelling for his readers.

Looking back at your childhood fan fiction writing at age eight, what lessons did those early stories teach you, and how did they shape your voice as a writer today?

To be honest, I look back at those stories (or rather the idea behind them) and things are very different now. I always loved the supernatural, superheroes – what kid doesn't ? But I always saw the questions in my head: "What would happen is X did Y?" I think it's one of the important things that any writer has to consider: even if it's not there, you should see that situation and wonder how your characters would react.

With an academic background in English Studies and experience in television advertising, how have those worlds influenced your storytelling style and creative process?

Your brain might tell you that the two worlds shouldn't interact at all – and to an extent, they shouldn't – but there's some crossover there. After all, what's the point of writing your book if you don't have an idea of how to market it, who your reader is.

That hasn't influenced my writing, but it has made me embrace the story, and I think it makes me a better writer. And it also meant I have little time for books or writers doing it just to get famous or make money.

You started out as a reviewer before becoming an author. What motivated that shift, and how did reviewing others' work affect how you approach your own?

Ken Mooney discusses his creative process, mythological fantasy worlds, LGBTQ+ themes, memoir writing, and the personal challenges that inspired his heartfelt and fearless literary legacy in this compelling interview.

Blending Fantasy, Life, And Identity

Ken Mooney Weaves Mythology, Memoir, And LGBTQ+ Tales Into Emotional And Captivating Worlds

I shifted because of a conflict of interests: it wasn't appropriate to attend a movie premier, write up a review…and then try to deliver an advertising campaign for same.

Godhead my first novel, was a story that had been floating in my head since I was a teenager and when I stepped away from reviewing and the likes, was very natural to go back and give myself the push I needed to get it out into the world.

Your series The Last Olympiad reimagines Greek gods in the modern world through a dark fantasy lens. What inspired you to blend mythology with horror, and what themes did you want to explore most?

I'm a big believer in not forcing a story – that may say more about myself than my work, and it works for me. When I was close to publishing Godhead, there had been some bereavement in the family, and a superhero/horror very naturally turned into a very human story about grief, family – and chosen family too. And when that came out, I couldn't put it away.

I think fantasy and horror can be frowned on, and usually by people who are very cold, or just don't get people. To me, all sorts of stories are analyses of the human condition and everything that comes with it….the good stuff and the bad.

You've written across diverse genres—from fantasy to memoir to LGBTQ romance. How do you adjust your creative mindset when switching between such different forms of storytelling?

I've never looked in depth at my own headspace, more that there's a story in there that needs to get out – and sometimes those voices are very loud!

For example, The Astrocytoma Diaries is my own of talking about being diagnosed with – and treated for – a brain tumour. There was so much going on that the only way I could deal with it was writing it down – a couple of hundred words allowing me to vent. Publishing was my way of closing off part of that journey – but putting it out there has allowed other people on similar journeys to read and get in touch. It's an honour that I've been able to give people some hope or support, or just know they're not alone.

Regarding my LGBTQ+ romance, I was teased by a fellow writer to give it a shot, and like my other works, the stories just sort of told themselves when I let them out. Tackling The Issue started as something romantic, but one character was very angry at the world and he just had to let it out. It's set shortly after the Irish Marriage Referendum of 2015, a time when myself and many others saw a level of support and respect that we would've never expected. But in amongst that joy and celebration, there was an anger too, wondering where that open support had been before. And some similar levels of anger, trust – and mistrust – are there in the shorts available in Trust Issues.

Kristen Martin

Kristen Martin discusses writing across genres, transformative personal growth, spiritual awakening, career-defining moments, and her exciting upcoming projects, showcasing her passion for storytelling and empowering creatives.

Kristen Martin, a powerhouse of creativity and determination, is truly an inspiration in the literary and entrepreneurial worlds. As an Amazon bestselling author, writing coach, content creator, and speaker, Kristen has carved a remarkable path that merges storytelling with personal growth, ambition, and authenticity. With an impressive catalog spanning over ten books across genres like YA fantasy, science fiction, and personal development, her ability to create captivating narratives and introspective explorations is nothing short of extraordinary. Each page Kristen writes is infused with unshakable passion, boundless imagination, and a deep understanding of human connection—a trio that has solidified her work as a beacon of inspiration for readers around the globe.

Exploring Genres, Personal Growth And Creative Evolution

Kristen Martin Inspires Through Storytelling and Creativity

In this feature, we delve into Kristen's creative journey and celebrate the brilliance behind her storytelling. From the intricate twists and turns of the *Shadow Crown* series to the deeply transformative experiences encapsulated in her self-help book *Soulflow*, Kristen's work demonstrates a rare versatility that transcends genres and inspires profound reflection. Whether she's immersing her readers into otherworldly realms or sharing her own heartfelt truths, her stories resonate deeply, leaving an indelible mark on readers' lives.

Beyond the pages, Kristen's role as a writing coach and creative entrepreneur showcases her commitment to empowering others to chase their dreams and unlock their own creative potential. Her YouTube and podcast platforms are shining examples of how she merges authenticity and expertise, motivating her audience to take bold strides toward living a life they love.

Mosaic Digest is proud to host this illuminating interview with Kristen, reflecting on her astonishing career, her evolutionary creative process, and her plans for what's next. Whether you're a writer seeking inspiration, a devoted fan of Kristen's work, or simply a lover of compelling storytelling, her insights offer an unforgettable glimpse into a mind brimming with creativity.

Midnight Reign brings the Shadow Crown series to a dramatic conclusion. What was the most challenging part of wrapping up such an expansive story?

The most challenging part of writing the final book in the Shadow Crown series was making sure the conclusion had that final "punch" I'd been working up to for so many years. Of course, it's crucial to make sure any and all foreshadowing is wrapped up so that the reader isn't left wondering with more questions than answers. But, overall, writing an ending that was not only satisfying but worthwhile was the most challenging part of wrapping up this story.

During the process of writing your self-help book, Soulflow, what was one discovery that deeply impacted you or changed your perspective?

The depth of self-reflection shocked me. Soulflow forced me to confront my darkest shadows and deepest fears and write about them in what would become a very public medium. Vulnerability has never been my strong suit, but it was such a cathartic process that I actually cried while writing the entire ending of that book. Needless to say, it left me forever changed.

Your standalone novel Beyond the Stars and Shadows blends metaphysical elements with a contemporary setting—what inspired you to tell your story through this unique lens?

During the time of writing Beyond the Stars and Shadows, I was in the midst of a spiritual awakening. The pull I felt to capture my experiences through a creative outlet was so strong that I began mapping out characters to symbolize what I was going through. It's such an introspective story, one that was written during a pivotal moment of my life, and I'm so glad I was able to convey my journey through that unique lens.

Looking back on your journey as an author, coach, and entrepreneur, what moment or milestone stands out as the most defining in your career?

There are honestly so many, but if I had to pick just one, it would be attending BookCon during my book tour across the U.S. I had the opportunity to meet so many readers and fans, and feeling that sense of community, connection, and shared love of reading and writing is something I'll carry with me for the rest of my life.

As you continue to grow creatively and professionally, what new directions or projects are you most excited to pursue next?

I have a few manuscripts in the works. One is an urban fantasy with paranormal elements, another is a YA romantic fantasy, and the other is a gothic thriller, which is a new genre I'm just now dabbling in. As for content creation, I plan to continue documenting my creative process and lifestyle in the hopes that it will inspire writers from all walks of life to write their books and get their voice out there.

JoAnn M. Dickinson

JoAnn M. Dickinson is a celebrated author whose children's books inspire and educate young readers by blending captivating adventures with meaningful life lessons. Her stories, often drawing from experiences with her grandchildren, explore themes like kindness, compassion, empathy, diversity, and the wonders of nature. With a focus on STEM, social-emotional learning (SEL), and auditory engagement, JoAnn's books help spark curiosity while nurturing a sense of self-discovery and learning in children.

We sat down with JoAnn to learn more about her creative journey and the impact her work has had on families around the world.

Multi-Award-Winning Author JoAnn M. Dickinson, known for her captivating children's books, celebrates storytelling that sparks imagination and lifelong learning.

Inspires Young Minds Through Enchanting Tales of Adventure and Learning

Celebrating Her Journey As A Multi-Award-Winning Children's Author

From Dream to Reality

JoAnn's journey as an author began with a moment of simple inspiration. "It all started with my grandson's first camping trip," she shares. "Witnessing his excitement and wonder as he explored nature motivated me to write *John's Camping Adventures*. It began as a simple story to capture that experience but grew into a passion I hadn't anticipated."

This pivotal moment not only launched JoAnn's first book but also set the course for a career in self-publishing. "I chose self-publishing to retain creative freedom and bring my stories to life on my timeline," she explains. Alongside a trusted team of editors, illustrators, and designers, JoAnn has built a body of work deeply rooted in creativity and intentionality. "Over time, my storytelling has become more purposeful, tackling themes like kindness, adventure, and STEM learning in ways that resonate with children."

The Inspiration Behind the Stories

JoAnn's most recent book, *Rory's Quest: A Lou's Zoo Adventure,* is the third installment in her popular *Lou's Zoo Series*. "This book follows the heartfelt journey of Rory, a young rhino searching for his lost mother," she shares. "Rory faces challenges, relies on friends, and discovers the strength within himself. His story is about perseverance, hope, and the importance of meaningful connections."

Through Rory's journey, JoAnn aims to leave a lasting message with her readers. "I hope families take away the power of resilience and the value of leaning on others for support, especially when facing life's unexpected challenges," she says.

Navigating Creativity and Business

As both an author and entrepreneur, JoAnn has faced the delicate balance of creativity and business. "The biggest challenge is dividing my time between writing and managing the ongoing demands of marketing," she explains. "While I love the creative process, I also need to promote my books, maintain a social media presence, attend book fairs, and connect with readers."

Although demanding, JoAnn has embraced this part of her career. "I've learned to prioritize my schedule and rely on my team when needed. The process has made me more resourceful and adaptable, and it's rewarding to see my stories reach children all over the world."

Encouraging Positivity and Learning

A hallmark of JoAnn's work is her focus on positivity, kindness, and enthusiasm for learning. "These are values I deeply believe in, and I incorporate them into my books naturally," she says. "But beyond that, I'm passionate about making science and nature exciting for children. My *Amelia Ophelia Series,* for example, introduces kids to topics like bee conservation and ocean protection in fun, approachable ways."

For JoAnn, storytelling is about more than entertainment. "I want children to feel empowered—to see how their curiosity and actions can make a difference. In today's fast-paced, tech-centric world, stories that nurture empathy and education are more important than ever."

Connecting with Readers

One of JoAnn's greatest joys is hearing from young readers and their families. "I've had kids tell me they've been inspired to go camping like John or dream of building rockets like Rylee," she shares with a smile. "It's these moments of connection that remind me why I write."

Feedback from her readers also influences her work. "I pay attention to the questions kids ask or the characters they relate to most. Their excitement often fuels my next idea. At the heart of it, my goal is to create stories that make every child feel seen, inspired, and encouraged to explore their potential."

ALYSSA MAXWELL

Inspires With Historical Mysteries That Blend Riveting Plots And Richly Detailed Worlds

BY MOSAIC DIGESTE STAFF

Alyssa Maxwell, a masterful storyteller and celebrated mystery author, has carved out a remarkable niche in the world of historical mysteries. With more than twenty books in print, Maxwell continues to captivate readers with her Gilded Newport Mysteries and A Lady & Lady's Maid Mysteries, blending rich period details, compelling characters, and intricately woven plots. Her debut novel, Murder at The Breakers—a USA Bestseller and now adapted into a Hallmark Mystery Channel movie—represents the start of a series that immerses readers in high-society intrigue alongside the gritty and determined sleuthing of Emma Cross. With themes that explore independence, community, and the resilience of women past and present, Maxwell's storytelling transports readers to gilded mansions and post-WWI English estates, threading her tales with wit, warmth, and clever twists.

As editor of Mosaic Digest magazine, it is our honor to feature Alyssa Maxwell in this special interview, where she reflects on her journey, her creative process, and the evolving lives of her beloved characters. Maxwell offers a fascinating glimpse into her Newport-inspired roots, shares the surreal experience of seeing her story come to life on screen, and delves into the challenges and joys of crafting dual narratives through aristocratic and working-class perspectives.

Whether you're a devoted fan of the genre or a newcomer intrigued by historical mysteries, Alyssa Maxwell's literary world is an invitation to travel through time, uncover secrets, and savor the artistry of her craft. Mosaic Digest celebrates her incredible impact on the literary world and welcomes readers to join us in discovering the layers of storytelling and connection that make her work truly extraordinary.

Your Gilded Newport Mysteries are inspired by your husband's multi generation family history in Newport. How did that personal connection shape the character of Emma Cross and the stories you chose to tell?

My personal experiences of being part of a Newport family, along with my husband's experiences of having grown up there, have allowed me to see the city on a deeper level and better understand the character and attitudes of the local populace. There is something unique about people who hail from islands. They tend to be fiercely independent, self-reliant, determined, stoic, and, at the same time, tightly bonded to their communities. I saw it in my in-laws; I see it in my husband, and I have tried to instill these qualities into Emma to make her a strong, resolute young woman uniquely positioned to solve what often seems unsolvable. Like my own mother-in-law, if Emma can help someone, she will, and if this takes her into dangerous situations, she draws on the strength which she believes originates from

---

Alyssa Maxwell shares insights into her journey as a bestselling mystery author, her characters' evolution, creative process, and community building, while exploring themes of independence, resilience, and societal change.

---

the very bedrock of Aquidneck Island.

As you celebrate your eleventh year as a published mystery author with over twenty titles so far, how have your creative process and approach to historical mystery evolved over that time?

I've learned to do a lot more preplanning. I'm always amazed when authors, especially mystery authors, say they don't sketch out a synopsis beforehand. Somehow, it works for them, but not for me. Writing a synopsis is hard work, but I've come to appreciate having that guide map when I sit down each day to write. But first, I flesh out my characters: who they are, what experiences have shaped the kind of people they are, and—most important for a mystery—what they might be hiding, whether it has to do with the murder or not. By now, I know my primary characters

as well as I know my real-life family, but each story comes with new secondary characters, both fictional and based in history, and I've learned I cannot plot a book until I understand them well enough to know how they'll react or be proactive in any given situation.

"Murder at The Breakers" was adapted into a Hallmark Mystery Channel movie four years after being discovered in Newport. What surprised you most when seeing your characters and setting transition from page to screen?

It was surreal seeing the characters I've lived with for over ten years move across the TV screen, speak words I wrote, and enact the scenarios I conceived. It's important to remember that a production studio will always put their own twist on the literary material they work with, and they made a couple of additions that I really applauded. One was the inclusion of the Tabbs Carriage Company, which existed in Newport at the time. Soon after the first airing I heard from a long-time Newporter who was a descendent of the man who founded that company, an example of a successful African American-owned business that thrived in Newport's relatively progressive atmosphere. Hearing from that individual was a joy to me, and to the screenwriter.

Your upcoming "Murder at Arleigh" (Gilded Newport Mysteries #13) is set for late August 2025. Without spoiling too much—what themes or new facets of Emma's life can readers expect to explore in this latest entry?

The biggest evolution in Emma's life is becoming a mother. We see her in this role for the first time in Murder at Arleigh, and we learn how she balances motherhood with her newspaper work, which she is not willing to give up. Then there is her sleuthing and the danger such activities might bring to her family and her precious daughter. She struggles at times with the prospect of having to step away and whether she's being selfish by accepting the challenge of finding a killer. But we also see how she has found a new source of strength in her family; how holding her daughter, spending time with her watching the ocean waves behind the house, or doing simple things like reading bedtime stories, act as a balm on her soul and renew her resolve.

In your Lady & Lady's Maid Mysteries, you pair Lady Phoebe with her maid Eva in post WWI England. How did you develop that dynamic duo, and what do you see as the strengths of telling a mystery through both perspectives?

The idea for this series actually came from my editor, who wanted to see "Downton Abbey with a mystery twist." This was in 2014 or so, when the show was at the height of its popularity. Being a huge fan, I jumped at the chance to create something similar—but different. Other than my editor wanting the dynamic of three sisters and a country estate setting, as in the TV series, I was given free rein in terms of characters, time period, etc. In my Newport series, Emma has a dual heritage, that of Vanderbilt and Newporter, allowing her to mix freely with different segments of society. In A Lady & Lady's Maid, having two sleuths, each with her own point of view, allows for a similar scenario, that of moving comfortably in different social situations. Phoebe, of course, investigates "above stairs," among the aristocrats, while Eva handles the servants and villagers. Having them work together and become friends also illustrated the social and economic changes taking place in England in the years following WWI.

You're active in writing communities like Mystery Writers of America and South Florida Fiction Writers, and live in South Florida after decades. How does your personal and local environment influence your work and your connection to readers and peers?

Having a sense of community with other writers is vitally important. It's a generous community, with writers helping each other in all phases of their careers, from beginner to bestseller. Even seasoned authors attend workshops (as well as give them) to stay fresh and keep the creative juices flowing. Spouses and friends can be supportive, and that's important, but no one understands the effort and heart that go into a book the way other authors do. Through the organizations I belonged to in South Florida, I learned to be a writer, to craft fiction, and to weather the ups and downs of what can be a fickle business. My greatest challenge right now is having moved from Florida after forty years. My husband and I now live in California, near our daughter, and I'm faced with having to rebuild that community. Yes, thanks to the internet I'll remain in touch with good friends, but I look forward to making new connections, face to face.

Alyssa Maxwell's passion for storytelling and meticulous craftsmanship elevates historical mysteries, making them evocative journeys through time and character.

Alyssa Maxwell, *the acclaimed author of Gilded Newport Mysteries, pictured creating timeless tales of intrigue and resilience from her California home.*

"

Writing a synopsis is hard work, but I've come to appreciate having that guide map when I sit down each day to write."

Alyssa Maxwell

Lisa Weldon Turns Journeys Into Stories That Inspire Change

Discover Themes Of Reinvention, Creativity, And Resilience

Lisa Weldon shares insights on writing, reinvention, and storytelling, from her memoir Twenty Pieces to her exploration of fiction, inspiring readers to embrace authenticity and personal growth.

BY MOSAIC DIGEST STAFF

Lisa Weldon's journey as an author is nothing short of extraordinary. Her remarkable ability to weave vivid storytelling with profound themes of reinvention and resilience has captured hearts around the world. A woman who carved her own path—literally—in the streets of Manhattan before extending her explorations to Paris, Istanbul, Shanghai, Panama City, and small-town Fairhope, Alabama, Lisa's unique approach to storytelling has enriched not only her own life but also the lives of her readers. With a vision rooted in courage and authenticity, Lisa doesn't merely tell stories; she invites readers to walk through the worlds she creates, experiencing reinvention alongside her characters.

At Mosaic Digest magazine, we celebrate voices that inspire, challenge, and uplift, and Lisa Weldon embodies all of these qualities and more. Her memoir, *Twenty Pieces,* is an honest and evocative account of a woman reclaiming her life through movement—both outwardly across spaces and inwardly into the depths of her personal struggles. Perhaps most impressive is the humanity that underpins her work. Whether she's chronicling the vibrancy of foreign cities or delving into the complexities of the Civil Rights era in her upcoming fiction manuscript, Lisa's writing is a beautiful reminder of how history, geography, and personal transformation intertwine.

Through this candid interview,

Lisa Weldon offers us glimpses into her creative process—the courage to lean into emotion, the discipline of crafting narratives from reality and imagination, and the willingness to embrace feedback and growth. As an editor, I am honored to present her captivating insights to our readers, and it is our hope that this feature inspires others to not only tell their stories but live them fully. Mosaic Digest magazine is proud to showcase Lisa Weldon's brilliance, and we eagerly await her next literary adventure.

At what point did you realise the story you wanted to tell with Twenty Pieces was no longer just a project, but something you had to share?

Quite honestly, not until one of Oprah's producers called and said they'd read about my reinvention story and invited me to participate in one of their shows.

How do you balance authenticity and imagination when creating characters: do you draw from real life, or are your characters largely inventions?

In my current manuscript, I base most of my characters on people I know—then I bend and stretch them into villains, heroines, or whoever the story requires.

Funny enough, I reached out to a high school friend—a retired attorney—for help untangling the laws and trials of 1969, the year my story takes place. She is now a character in my story who plays a major role!

Can you describe a moment in your writing process where you felt stuck, and how you managed to move past it?

In my first years of writing, I worked with a Jane, a retired English professor who also had an M.A. in psychology. That psychology came in handy in getting me through some major roadblocks.

One major block came in year five. I was

Photo: *Lisa Weldon, author of Twenty Pieces, channels personal reinvention and global journeys into captivating, unforgettable stories.*

Photo by Emma Weldon

Photo: *Lisa Weldon strolling confidently through a vibrant New York City street, capturing the essence of urban life and personal exploration in her transformative journey.*

Photo by Joe Benton

tired and convinced my manuscript was good enough to send out. Jane warned me, "You're not ready." I didn't want to hear it. I sent out a query anyway, and four days later the agent wrote back: "I really wanted to love this story, but you're not ready."

I admitted to Jane what I'd done, and she fired me! Yep, fired me for not listening to her.

What rituals or habits help you maintain momentum during writing? Do you have a writing schedule, preferred environment, or particular tools?

My book is built around a 30-day walk

Lisa Weldon transforms personal journeys into meaningful narratives, inspiring readers with her courage, creativity, and heartfelt storytelling brilliance.

---

through Manhattan. I taped 30 index cards to my living room wall—one for each neighborhood I walked—and wrote my thoughts into the "container" of Day Six or Day Twenty. Breaking the story into small pieces made it less daunting.

I write best when I get away—alone—to a residency, the beach, or the mountains. At home, laundry and garden weeds pull me away the page.

Your narratives often explore themes of reinven-

tion and personal change — what draws you to those themes, and how have they played out in your own life?

I began writing—actually, journaling—as a way to heal from a major trauma in my life. I was raised in an era where the unspoken rule was to "get over it"— be strong, don't dwell on losses or disappointments. But as I've grown older, I've come to see that true healing doesn't come from brushing pain aside. To reach a "happy ending"—in a book or in life—you must walk through the hard times, face the emotions, and let them do their work. That process is what allows reinvention, and it's a theme that continues to shape both my writing and my life.

How does setting influence your stories? Do you "walk" through places (literally or figuratively) to get a sense of them for your writing?

In my current manuscript I explore the friendship of two young girls during the Civil Rights era. To capture the time, I've spent hours in archives. I've driven the back roads of South Alabama where the story is set, attended a Black church service to absorb cadence and language, and wandered through a historic cemetery looking for character names. A monthlong residency in Fairhope, Alabama allowed me to interview elders who recalled school integration firsthand. I even revisited my childhood home and the creek behind it, the place where I base my story.

How do reviews, reader feedback, or criticism affect your work, both during drafting and after publication?

I appreciate ANYONE who listens to my story and helps me improve it! "Two sets of eyes" are always better than one.

Was there a piece of advice or a particular author/book that significantly shaped your approach to writing or storytelling?

"Just vomit the words," Jane would remind me again and again. As a perfectionist, I often tripped over my own need to polish too soon.

One book that encouraged me was Wild by Cheryl Strayed. I'll never forget—I was boarding a plane to go on a 30-day walk of Paris when a friend called and said, "Oprah just announced a new book called Wild. It's your story!"

What are you working on next, and in what ways is it similar or different from your previous work?

My first book was memoir. My second is fiction—a big leap! In the memoir, I simply recorded events that happened. With this one, I must build the story completely from scratch. It's harder in so many ways, but also much more fun—I get to let my creativity run wild.

For other emerging authors: what one piece of advice would you give them to help them stay true to their voice while also developing craft, discipline, and resilience in the often-challenging publishing process?

"Don't write to publish, or to please agents, publishers, or readers. Write to please YOU!"

Exploring Displacement And Belonging In A Divided World

MONA KAMAL

Mona Kamal Illuminates Migration and Identity Through Art

In this interview, Mona Kamal explores themes of migration, identity, religion, and conflict, sharing her deeply personal art practice that connects family stories, history, and global struggles to spark empathy.

Mona Kamal is a bold force in contemporary art, a creator whose work seamlessly melds the personal and political to narrate migration, identity, and the human condition. Over her two-decade career, Mona has crafted a unique space where personal histories resonate within the broader contexts of global struggles. Her powerful multimedia installations and video works challenge audiences to confront the legacies of displacement, grapple with the complexities of belonging, and explore the scars left by geopolitical and cultural divides. Mona's talent lies not just in her technical skill or innovative use of media, but in her ability to uncover universal truths through deeply personal experiences, creating an artistic voice that echoes far beyond the gallery walls.

Rooted in exploration, dialogue, and a desire for connection, Mona's work often integrates familial stories, historical artifacts, and traditional motifs to evoke profound emotional response. As a product of her migratory upbringing and cross-cultural experience, her artistic practice navigates the symbolic and literal borders of nationhood and memory. Whether through large-scale installations, paper-plane creations, or immersive video performances, Mona Kamal's art invites audiences to journey into shared histories and a common humanity that transcends divisions of geography, culture, and religion. Through exhibitions spanning continents—from Canada and India to New York and Pakistan—her work has become a global anthem for urgent topics: the complexities of identity, the sting of systemic inequality, and the often-overlooked consequences of war.

Mona Kamal's work is as visceral as it is visual—engaging viewers, spurring participati-

Mona Kamal's "13 Years 7 Months 6 Days" is a poignant and visually arresting installation that transforms historical tragedy into evocative art. Comprising 429 intricately painted paper planes suspended from the ceiling, the work signifies the drone attacks in Waziristan over the specified length of time. The overwhelming density of the planes and their stark precision evoke a visceral response—a haunting weight of loss and memory. Kamal's meticulous process and concept showcase her mastery in fusing personal narrative with global issues, making this project both deeply moving and universally significant.

on, and fostering dialogue. In this interview, she provides rare insight into the inspirations behind her creations, offering an unfiltered glimpse into her process, themes, and passion for dismantling narratives of marginalization.

Describing her deeply personal yet globally

> Mona Kamal's art transcends borders with powerful storytelling, transforming deeply personal experiences into universal truths of identity and belonging.

significant video project *Border Crossing* (2013), Mona speaks to the complexities of migration and identity. This piece documents her journey across the border from Pakistan to India, a site forged during the 1947 Partition of British India—a cataclysmic event that displaced millions. The video juxtaposes the geographic division with striking similarities between the two nations. As Mona recounts, "The people look the same, speak the same language, and it's clear how futile the partition was." Yet, her project is more than historical commentary; it's an exploration of her own place within this fractured past. Through her struggle with language and distinct cultural attire, the video underscores her feeling of being a visitor in lands she is ancestrally tied to but does not inhabit—an epitome of the migrant's struggle with belonging.

A recurring thread in Mona Kamal's work is her use of familial stories and historical artifacts, which serve as gateways to forgotten histories. From manuscripts and photographs sourced during her travels to Pakistan and India, these fragments of her family's life before the Partition reflect the longing for a "missing link" lost to history. However, this search often deepens her sense of disconnect. "So few photos and

memories remain of a time when my family was together," she shares, "and this absence is at the core of my work."

More recently, her practice has included found objects from her Brooklyn neighborhood as a way to evoke nostalgia and connection to a bygone era. These artifacts infuse her creations with a tactile sense of history—pieces that invite viewers to reflect on the fragile threads that tether personal narratives to collective memory.

One of Mona Kamal's most provocative works, *Drones in Waziristan,* transforms cold statistics into a poignant call for empathy. This installation features a carpet embroidered with the date of every drone attack in Pakistan, symbolizing the physical and emotional wounds inflicted by the so-called "War on Terror." Exhibition attendees are prompted to walk across the carpet—a deliberate act that echoes the disregard and invisibility often imposed upon those most affected by war.

Currently, Mona is creating 429 paper planes—one for each drone attack in Pakistan. The planes, suspended above audiences, evoke the oppressive fear and trauma war civilians endure. "It's about creating a heaviness," she explains. "I want viewers to feel what it might be like to live under the constant presence of drones—to hear, to see, to never know if you'll be next." This immersive element is central to Mona's philosophy: art must engage the senses and challenge perceptions to inspire understanding and awareness.

Religion and its intersection with conflict is another recurring theme in Mona's work. In her 2014 piece, *The Women,* she engraved a chapter of the Quran—"The Women"—onto shapes meant to signify burqa-clad figures. This piece strikes at the heart of the stereotypes and narratives surrounding Islam, aiming to create dialogue about the ways both the East and the

West perpetuate oversimplified views of the region and its people.

For Mona, religion is never discussed in isolation but against the backdrop of identity and belonging. Her migratory experiences lend her a lens that is uniquely nuanced—shaped by years of crossing cultures, borders, and ideologies. "I've never felt I belonged to one place," she reflects. "Nationalism, for me, has little to do with borders and everything to do with culture and community." It is through this lens, one of displacement and solidarity, that her art speaks so powerfully to those on the margins.

Mona Kamal's work is a vivid testament to the power of art in fostering understanding and dismantling division. Her storytelling builds bridges—connecting audiences to forgotten histories, unspoken pains, and marginalized voices. Whether probing the scars of colonialism, exploring the plight of war's forgotten victims, or evoking the universal longing for home and belonging, Mona's art demands to be seen, felt, and understood.

In a world fractured by divides—of nations, religions, and ideologies—Mona Kamal reminds us of our shared humanity and the responsibility we hold to one another. Her creations serve as a call to empathy, an invitation to reflect, and a spark for change—a lasting proof of creativity's ability to illuminate the shadows and build a more compassionate world.

KRISTEL BALDOZ

> Kristel Baldoz's innovative artistry masterfully challenges norms, explores profound themes with courage, and inspires transformative dialogue in contemporary art.

Art & Media

Kristel Baldoz Pushes Boundaries Through Multidisciplinary Art

Kristel Baldoz's art challenges societal structures, plays with object animacy, and reflects immigrant labor and femininity through ceramics, dance, and performance works.

Kristel Baldoz, a New York City-based multidisciplinary artist of Filipina-American heritage, is a rising force in contemporary art, celebrated for her evocative and innovative approach to exploring themes of identity, labor, materiality, and power. Using a combination of dance, performance, and ceramics, her work transcends conventional artistic boundaries, confronting deeply rooted societal structures while inviting audiences into a space of introspection.

Raised in Delano, California—a community steeped in the history of migrant labor activism and the historic Table Grape Strike led by Larry Itliong and Cesar Chavez—Kristel's art is profoundly shaped by her upbringing. Her parents, former immigrant farmworkers, inspire her work with their stories of resilience and labor in the fields. "From a young age,

I witnessed the repetitive and monotonous motion of picking grapes, an act that illustrates the invisibilization of immigrant labor," Kristel shares.

This intimate understanding of the intersection between identity and labor informs her art. Kristel channels the physicality and rhythm of her family's work into her experimentation with dance, connecting it to the broader landscape of racialized histories and the multifaceted, often unseen labor of Asian women. Her heritage becomes not only a foundation for her art but also a lens through which she interrogates power structures and cultural narratives.

A cornerstone of Kristel's artistic vision is "indictment"—using art to confront and draw attention to the unseen and unspoken. Through silence and abstraction in her work, she reclaims agency from colonial and gendered fetishizations. In her performance *Yellow*

Kristel Baldoz's Yellow Fever masterfully interrogates the intersection of femininity, orientalism, and objectification through a multidisciplinary lens. Drawing from Anne Anlin Cheng's concept of ornamentalism, Baldoz blurs the lines between objecthood and personhood. The performance's meticulous choreography and integration of ceramics explore the fetishization of the female Asian identity, demanding viewers to confront societal constructs. The evocative use of translucent materials, geometric forms, and movement transforms the stage into a space of indictment and transformation. Yellow Fever is a bold, thought-provoking statement on identity, agency, and resilience.

Fever, Kristel employs silence as a powerful form of communication, subverting stereotypes of Asian female docility. "It is a silence that demands to be heard," she explains, challenging audiences to listen to what cannot be ignored.

For Kristel, objects in her work are not mere props but active participants in her storytelling. Drawing on Anne Anlin Cheng's concept of Ornamentalism, she explores the fetishization of Asian women, often likened to ornamental objects. By intentionally blurring the lines between objecthood and person-

Kristel Baldoz exemplifies bold creativity, masterfully reimagining narratives, breaking boundaries, and inviting transformative reflection through her provocative and multifaceted artistry.

hood, Kristel critiques the dehumanizing aspects of colonialism and identity politics.

Her performances and sculptures reframe objects by imbuing them with agency. For example, in *Yellow Fever*, she uses ceramic wigs and cinder blocks to reimagine these items as symbols of fragility and power. The ceramic wig becomes a persona that interrogates the objectification of Asian women, while the cinder blocks, traditionally recognized for their strength, are recontextualized as fragile, poetic objects. In creating and animating these objects, Kristel liberates them from their colonial and patriarchal associations.

Kristel's practice is deeply tied to the histories of labor, colonialism, and femininity, particularly as they relate to immigrant experiences. Her personal history connects with larger global and historical narratives, from the legacy of farmworkers in Delano to the export labor trends shaped by colonial systems in the Philippines. "Export labor was born of colonialism: sending Filipinos to other countries to perform labor that is tied to the economic landscape of the Philippines," she says.

Through her art, Kristel prompts reflection on these realities, challenging the audience to consider the historical and modern-day implications of systems that exploit labor, particularly that of women and immigrants.

Rather than telling a linear or narrated story, Kristel employs abstraction and absurdity, intending to create an active dialogue between her art and its audience. Dance, one of her chosen mediums, plays a pivotal role in this process. "Dance is incredibly powerful in its ability to conjure a unique, visceral experience—one which both evades and engages with narration," Kristel notes.

By eschewing traditional storytelling, Kristel allows her audience to approach her art through their own perspectives and experiences, creating space for reflection on critical issues such as colonialism, immigration, and identity. Her priority, she says, is cultivating an experiential connection—one that leaves a lasting impression rooted in the audience's memory.

As an artist, Kristel Baldoz continues to

receive recognition from prestigious institutions, including New York University's Production Lab, New York Live Arts, Jonah Bokaer Arts Foundation, and Brooklyn Arts Exchange. Her art is both a call to action and an invitation to reflect, as it redefines the boundaries of multidisciplinary art. At its core, her work celebrates the transformative power of creativity, challenging audiences to confront societal systems of marginalization and recognize the resilience behind often invisible narratives.

Through her evocative use of materials, movement, and meaning, Kristel reframes inherited histories, creating deeply thought-provoking works with a revolutionary sense of agency. Both poetic and provocative, her art is a testament to her commitment to challenging the status quo and envisioning new possibilities for art and identity. In a world where labor, identity, and power are deeply intertwined, Kristel Baldoz is a shining example of how contemporary artists are reshaping the cultural dialogue with courage, creativity, and authenticity.

Blending Textiles, Technology, and Tradition With Humor and Vibrant Storytelling

> "
> Each stitch connects me to crafting women who were overlooked as artists."

HALE EKİNCİ

Hale Ekinci Weaves Heritage and Innovation Into Contemporary Fiber Art

Hale Ekinci blends textiles, photography, and embroidery into vibrant works that explore identity, heritage, gendered labor, and belonging with humor, innovation, and a deep connection to her immigrant experience.

Hale Ekinci stands as a beacon of artistic ingenuity—championing a unique fusion of cultural exploration, bold storytelling, and material innovation. A Turkish-American artist, Ekinci's work bridges the past and present, blending Middle Eastern and Western traditions while navigating the complexities of identity, immigration, and belonging. Through her striking artworks, she transforms ordinary household textiles into extraordinary creations, stitching together narratives laden with memory, culture, and defiance. Whether through her richly embroidered paintings, playful sculptural installations, or evocative video projects, Ekinci's practice is as experimental as it is deeply personal.

Her work carries a vibrant duality—a blend of digital precision and the tactile intimacy of hand-stitched embroidery. Ekinci's ability to utilize humor, symbolism, and improvisation allows her to challenge societal norms while celebrating themes of gendered labor, heritage, and collective memory. Her artistic process, rooted in both traditional craft and contemporary technology, reveals an intricate and imaginative world, a world that is as joyous as it is thought-provoking.

As Ekinci explains, her journey into fiber art began with a need for balance. Being a full-time graphic design professor and a seasoned animator required long hours in front of a computer. To counterbalance this rigid, digital work, Ekinci found herself drawn to the tactile satisfaction of knitting and crocheting. A short embroidery workshop at the ACRE artist residency solidified her passion, triggering a creative transformation where her past knowledge of solvent photo transfer techniques merged with her newfound appreciation for textiles and digital tools. "For me, it came out of a bodily need for a tactile process and joy," she reflects.

A hallmark of Ekinci's work is her distinctive practice of transferring old family photographs onto repurposed household textiles. This process becomes a way to translate memory into something tangible and enduring. Whether the photographs belong to her own Turkish heritage, her Indiana-born husband, or archival imagery of immigrants and queer individuals throughout history, Ekinci removes the settings to create figures that exist in a timeless, placeless realm. She uses a method involving wintergreen oil, applying it to printed photographs and transferring the imagery to the fabric's surface with careful precision. The result is a fluid merging of the past and the present that centers on the people and their stories, leaving the surrounding contexts deliberately open to interpretation.

Bridging her expertise in art and computer science, Ekinci incorporates digital tools into almost every stage of her creative process. Her background allows her to

Hale Ekinci's work stands out as an extraordinary fusion of tradition, innovation, and personal narrative. In New New House, Ekinci transforms ordinary textiles into vibrant, layered creations. Her seamless blend of hand-stitched embroidery, digital techniques, and cultural symbolism challenges conventions while celebrating identity, memory, and humor. With intricate textures, bold patterns, and imaginative storytelling, she invites viewers into a deeply personal yet universally resonant exploration of belonging and heritage. Her craftsmanship sparks thought and joy in equal measure.

Hale Ekinci's bold artistry challenges conventions while celebrating identity, culture, and history through mesmerizing, innovative fiber and multimedia works.

---

quickly adopt new creative software and push the boundaries of what can be done with fiber art. She relies on digital platforms like Photoshop and her iPad to sketch ideas, experiment with colors and patterns, and envision potential designs for her textiles. Recently, during her residency at Indiana University Bloomington, Ekinci utilized a large-format fabric printer to develop her own digital patterns, which she then printed directly onto textiles. This ability to mesh traditional handcrafting with high-tech tools reflects not only her innovative spirit but also her commitment to evolving her practice. Additionally, her digital proficiency extends to documenting her work, building her website, and managing her digital marketing—elements that give her greater creative autonomy.

Hand-embroidery holds deep meaning for Ekinci, both within the context of her artworks and on a personal level. It plays a pivotal role in completing the story of her pieces, acting as outlines, embellishments, and layers of cultural symbolism. "Embroidery often comes later," she explains. After transferring photographs and painting over them, she uses embroidery details to invoke an additional layer of narrative. Through meticulous hand-stitching, Ekinci invites viewers into a dynamic interplay of identity, memory, and humor. French knots obscure the faces in her embroidered portraits, ad-

ding anonymity, mystery, and a sense of universal connection. She uses cultural symbols—Turkish fezzes, tea cups, party hats, prayer beads—to challenge assumptions and imagine alternative narratives. Heteronormative men might adorn themselves with flower crowns reminiscent of Frida Kahlo, while a Turkish villager might hold an embroidered solo cup once reserved for American college parties.

Every stitch connects Ekinci with her personal history and lineage—her mother, neighbors, and the many generations of women whose craft has been overlooked by traditional artistic hierarchies. "Besides this emotional and political devotion to it, I also love how it makes me feel: how the slow stabbing of the fiber feels, how the colors accumulate, and how carrying it with me wherever I go makes me feel immersed in my creativity all the time," she shares.

Over the past few years, Ekinci has experienced a period of remarkable creative productivity. For her, the key has been finding structure within an organic process. She describes her methodology as a "recipe" that allows her to work intuitively: collecting printed photographs, choosing from her vast array of patterned textiles, transferring images, painting, embroidery, block printing, and adding crochet edges. This structured approach has freed her from self-doubt or overthinking, opening space to listen to the materials and let them guide her. Working with textiles also bestows a unique flexibility on her practice. She can embroider at home, on the couch, or during social events—extending her creative time. Concentrated residencies, like those at Spudnik Printmaking Press and Indiana University Bloomington, have also provided her with the time and resources to

dedicate herself fully to her craft.

Improvisation plays a vital role in Ekinci's creative process, particularly during the embroidery stage. In her practice, she sees each added embellishment as an opportunity to reimagine her subjects and their stories. For instance, in her sculptural piece *New New House*, she redefines traditional figures by introducing whimsical twists: a Turkish villager woman sporting acrylic nails, a solemn husband holding a solo cup, or a vintage American woman adorned with a Turkish prayer bead. These embroidered elements do more than add whimsy—they complicate preconceived narratives about culture and identity, creating a space to laugh, question, and connect with history on a personal level.

Hale Ekinci's work transcends the boundaries of tradition and technology, transforming ordinary fabrics into profound reflections of identity, memory, and connectivity. With each French knot, each painted flourish, and each digital design, she weaves her immigrant experience with a vibrant defiance that resonates universally. Her ability to incorporate joy, care, and self-discovery into every thread is nothing short of inspiring. Through her art, Hale Ekinci challenges us to see the layers in ourselves and others—not just as individuals, but as part of a collective human story. With every stitch, she embarks on an imaginative journey, crafting a world built on both heritage and innovation. And in doing so, she offers us a brilliant reminder: that even the ordinary fabrics of life can be transformed into something extraordinary.

Exploring Craft And Technology In Contemporary Art

KATE BURKE

Kate Burke Weaves Spirituality, Digital Influence, And Human Intimacy Into Mesmerizing Art

Kate Burke's art bridges tactile craft and digital influence, addressing themes of spirituality, identity, and emotional connection in innovative textiles and ceramics that transform digital experiences into tangible narratives.

Kate Burke stands at the crossroads of tradition and technology, weaving spirituality, digital influence, and the human condition into mesmerizing works of art. Based in Atlanta, Burke is a musician, artist, and performer whose creative practice bridges the tactile intimacy of textiles and ceramics with the ephemeral nature of contemporary digital culture. Her work is an exploration of belief systems, identity, and metaphysical poetry, offering viewers a unique lens through which to interrogate the intersections of these themes within our collective experiences both online and offline. With exhibitions in prestigious spaces like the Museum of Contemporary Art of Georgia and the Atlanta Contemporary, Kate Burke has earned esteemed recognition, including the ArtFields Category Award for

textiles and numerous fellowships such as her current role with The Creatives Project Residency. Her ability to integrate craft materials with deeply philosophical inquiry transforms her art into something fascinating and thought-provoking, challenging viewers to not only observe but engage, question, and confront unseen dynamics shaping their reality.

Burke's upbringing in Southern Baptist culture has profoundly influenced her artistic themes and exploration of spirituality throughout her body of work. She shares that her religious background and subsequent deconstruction of belief systems shaped the foundation of her artistic practice. It became important for her to acknowledge her upbringing while connecting it to broader human experiences. The rise of social media and its effect on identity and belief intersected with Burke's journey during her university years, rewiring how she approached concepts of spirituality and self-identification. Within her art, Burke draws on these personal experiences to question and reinterpret the role of belief and connection in a digitized, contemporary world.

Burke views the Internet as inherently spiritual. She reflects on how removing the physical devices—computers, phones, or tablets—would leave individuals with behaviors akin to prayer and devotion: focused, personal acts of engagement. This dichotomy of the physical and non-physical aspects of online connection became a focal point in her work. Burke was drawn to tactile materials such as textiles, ceramics, and craft, emphasizing that these mediums demand time as a resource, much like the "bandwidth" people devote to the digital realm. Through the fusion of intention, attention, and effort in craft practices, Burke acknowledges the ways digital language mirrors human experience—even if people aren't always conscious of this connection. She finds humor in how metaphysical poetry's historic exploration of dichotomies, paradoxes, and analytical thought aligns with her modern commentary on digital technology and craft. In particular, her play on contemporary terms such as "Meta" highlights the cyclical nature of human exploration through both tangible and intangible mediums.

The concepts of control, sin, and sel-

Kate Burke's visionary artistry merges profound intellectual depth with innovative craftsmanship, offering transformative reflections on technology and the human condition.

In this captivating box construction, Margo Klass demonstrates her masterful ability to create sacred spaces through found objects. The piece features a central bird figure perched contemplatively, framed by natural elements like twigs and branches that extend vertically along the sides. The artist's signature style of combining medieval altarpiece influence with Japanese aesthetic sensibilities is evident in the balanced composition and thoughtful use of space and light.

The earthy color palette and varied textures - from smooth surfaces to rough branches - create a harmonious dialogue between the natural and crafted elements. A hanging bell and window-like backdrop add depth and spiritual symbolism. This piece exemplifies Klass's talent for transforming ordinary objects into meditative sanctuaries that invite viewers to pause and reflect..

f-acceptance manifest deeply in Burke's artistic practice, shaped by both her religious upbringing and her experiences in the secular, digital sphere. She draws parallels between religious institutions dictating "truth" and the forces that shape digital experiences, such as misinformation, algorithms, and the psychology of social validation through engagement metrics. In Burke's view, the commodification of social identity, driven by capitalized platforms like Instagram, evokes feelings of "without," synonymous with the word "sin." These parallels reveal how technology amplifies the same insecurities and existential insecurities often associated with religious teachings, showing an ironic connection between disparate domains.

Burke's use of textiles and ceramics is key to her exploration of philosophical ideas, serving as grounding mediums that connect ancient human intimacy and technology to modern digital experiences. The tangible, intimate nature of textiles and ceramics allows her to make her digitized, ephemeral ideas physical, prompting viewers to engage with the intangible aspects of the human experien-

ce in real time. She hopes individuals recognize how their mental landscapes—formed through environments of connection, belief, and technology—manifest physically. Her art visualizes these dynamics and invites audiences to confront how shaping their existence in a digital sphere impacts their reality.

Through her transition from ethereal textile works to heavier ceramic mosaics, Burke plays with human expectations. Cementing weightless, digital imagery into solid, abrasive objects creates charged energy and redefines the viewer's relationship with digital experiences. Her long-term goal is to transmute digital ideas into both light, ethereal forms and heavy, intense mediums, acknowledging the full emotional and physical spectrum of digital engagement. A forthcoming exhibition in January will juxtapose the ethereal qualities of textiles with the gravity

of ceramic works, exploring the equilibrium between the delicacy and weight of digital experiences.

Burke underscores the profound effect of environment and cultural context in shaping an individual's emotional and spiritual disposition. Like experiments whose outcomes depend on external variables, she views environments—spiritual, mental, digital, and physical—as symbiotic or detrimental forces that inform her art. Her work teases out the mystery of how intangible experiences affect the physical realm, bringing these phenomena into the tangible plane of art for viewers to consider and reckon with. Ultimately, Burke's art grapples with questions of control, connection, and self-acceptance, contextualized through her unique fusion of craft and philosophy in a technology-driven age.

Dissecting Symbols, Media, And Spiritual Paradoxes

Karin Ferrari, celebrated artist and cultural detective, investigates the mystical undercurrents of media and consumer culture through her multidisciplinary practice.

KARIN FERRARİ

Karin Ferrari Explores Media, Mysticism And Hidden Visual Narratives

Karin Ferrari explores media, mysticism, and cultural narratives through art, deconstructing symbols in consumer culture, fringe theories, and architecture, while engaging audiences in critical thought about belief and visual influence.

Karin Ferrari is an artist who sees the unseen, a cultural decoder whose work reveals the hidden layers within the images we are constantly surrounded by. Fearless and innovative, she immerses herself into the intersections of consumerism, mysticism, and digital culture, peeling back the surface of media and cultural symbols to explore what lies beneath. Whether through her videos, installations, or prints, Ferrari challenges our perceptions of the world and lifts the curtain on the overlooked, the esoteric, and the bizarre.

Based in curiosity and inquiry, Ferrari's artistic vision dissects the culture of conspiracy and spirituality in an era shaped by the internet. Her term "trash mysticism" strikes at the heart of one of her central concerns: How mystical and symbolic ideas are democra-

tized, distorted, and disseminated in online culture, often taking on a life of their own. In her widely acclaimed DECODING (THE WHOLE TRUTH) series, Ferrari explores how belief systems and visual culture are interwoven, demonstrating how symbols, hidden messages, and cultural narratives help shape how we see the world. Her art invites us to question what we know and challenges us to reconsider the narratives we consume daily.

Ferrari's artistic journey took an important turn fourteen years ago, during what she describes as "the gilded age of YouTube." Late one night, her video recommendation feed transitioned into a peculiar library of conspiracy theories and fringe ideas presented in amateur, low-budget productions. Videos of reptilian shapeshifters and esoteric analyses of pop celebrities caught her attention—not only for their content but for the

A Techno-Magical Portal

Karin Ferrari's A Techno-Magical Portal is a mesmerizing videoinstallation that delves into the intersections of technology and mysticism. Exhibited at the Ferdinandeum Innsbruck in 2019, this work immerses viewers in a vibrant, futuristic atmosphere, where bold colors and dynamic visual elements create a sense of discovery and transcendence. The interplay of abstract visuals and modern design engages the audience, inviting introspection into the symbolic and spiritual undertones of digital media. Ferrari's mastery of creating immersive environments underscores her ability to transform media into a profound sensory and intellectual experience. This is a powerful commentary on our interconnected, digital existence.

visceral belief they prompted, even fleetingly. "For a moment, I believed," she recalls, "and it shifted my world." That moment of belief became the catalyst for her decision to turn such fringe cultural phenomena into art.

The DECODING series, Ferrari explains, is influenced by those videos and the questions they inspired: Why would consumer culture, ostensibly a rational and profit-driven system, lean so heavily into mysticism and symbolic imagery? Hidden themes in music videos, advertisements, and even news broadcasts

---

Karin Ferrari's insightful, innovative artistry boldly confronts the intersection of media, symbolism, and spirituality with extraordinary wit.

---

fascinated her. Her works explore how religious and archetypal motifs—from ancient Egyptian sun gods to devilish Earth goddesses—are infiltrating modern media and consumer spaces. In one video, Ferrari unpacks how Lady Gaga's music videos use mystical symbolism to depict her rise to superstardom.

In another, she examines the use of divine metaphors in smartphone advertisements, all while investigating hierarchies, celebrity worship, and their ties to capitalism.

Ferrari approaches such themes with equal parts humor, rigor, and critical analysis. Her work transcends mere parody by delving deep into what she calls "DIY mysticism" and the power of paranoia. "It's the joy of making sense of things," she explains, pointing out how humans routinely reshape their realities based on beliefs and frameworks—often without recognizing their influence. Artists, Ferrari argues, have a unique role to play in this conversation: They can freely explore ambiguity, contradiction, and irony, inviting audiences into a space of questioning and reflection.

Her exploration of pseudo-sacred commercial architecture in her project *Archi_Fictions of Ecstasy* is another fascinating dimension of her work. Drawing inspiration from research trips in South East Asia and cities like Manhattan, Ferrari investigates how mystical motifs subtly embed themselves into everyday spaces—hotels, shopping malls, financial towers. She highlights the architectural language of power and mysticism, describing what she calls "Rooftop Temples of New York City," where religious-like symbolism perches atop skyscrapers. For Ferrari, this blending of spirituality and commerce speaks

volumes about the desires and ideologies that underpin contemporary society.

As the media landscape grows more saturated—and distinctions between truth and fiction blur—Ferrari's work feels more urgent than ever. She invites her audience to interrogate their relationship with imagery and consider their role as participants in visual culture. "Let's create stories and narratives that inspire nice realities," she suggests, underscoring the symbolic and practical power of storytelling.

Looking ahead, Ferrari is set to exhibit at Verdurin, a project space in East London, in January. This new exhibition will focus on the aesthetics of conspiracy theories, a natural extension of her ongoing interests. While in London, she plans to study the city's financial architecture, continuing her exploration of how symbolism shapes economic and cultural power.

Karin Ferrari's blend of critical inquiry and imaginative storytelling positions her as a cultural visionary for the digital age. At a time when beliefs, myths, and images collide in increasingly complex ways, Ferrari takes us on a journey into the uncomfortable and the uncanny—where truth, fiction, and wonder meet.

Revealing Truths Through "Intentional Errors"

JOHN HILLIARD

John Hilliard Redefines Photography Through Intentional Imperfection

John Hilliard's innovative use of photography challenges conventional notions of perfection, embracing errors like blur and overexposure to explore truth, representation, and the transient nature of reality.

John Hilliard is a monumental figure in contemporary art, celebrated for his groundbreaking work that merges photography and sculpture to challenge our perceptions of reality. Born in Lancaster in 1945 and educated at London's prestigious St Martin's School of Art, Hilliard has spent decades reshaping the boundaries of photographic representation. His career is marked by a relentless exploration of photography not merely as a tool for documentation but as a profound medium worthy of deep investigation.

Hilliard's artistic journey began with site-specific installations in the United States, but it was his pivot to photography that solidified his reputation as a visionary artist. His work is characterized by intentional "errors" such as motion blur, variable focus, and multiple exposures—techniques that force viewers to reconsider the concept of the "perfect" image. These elements, often dismissed as technical flaws, are instead celebrated by Hilliard, highlighting the intrinsic qualities that make photography a unique and expressive art form.

In a recent interview with *WOWwART* magazine, Hilliard offered insights into his creative process and the philosophical underpinnings of his work. When asked about the influence of his early use of photography for documenting sculptures, Hilliard noted, "In recording my own work as a student at St Martin's in the Sixties, I was aware of the inevitable difference between the photograph and its object. This awareness prompted an interrogation of the medium, which has shaped all the work I've made since."

Hilliard's experimentation with the materials and instruments of photography is both

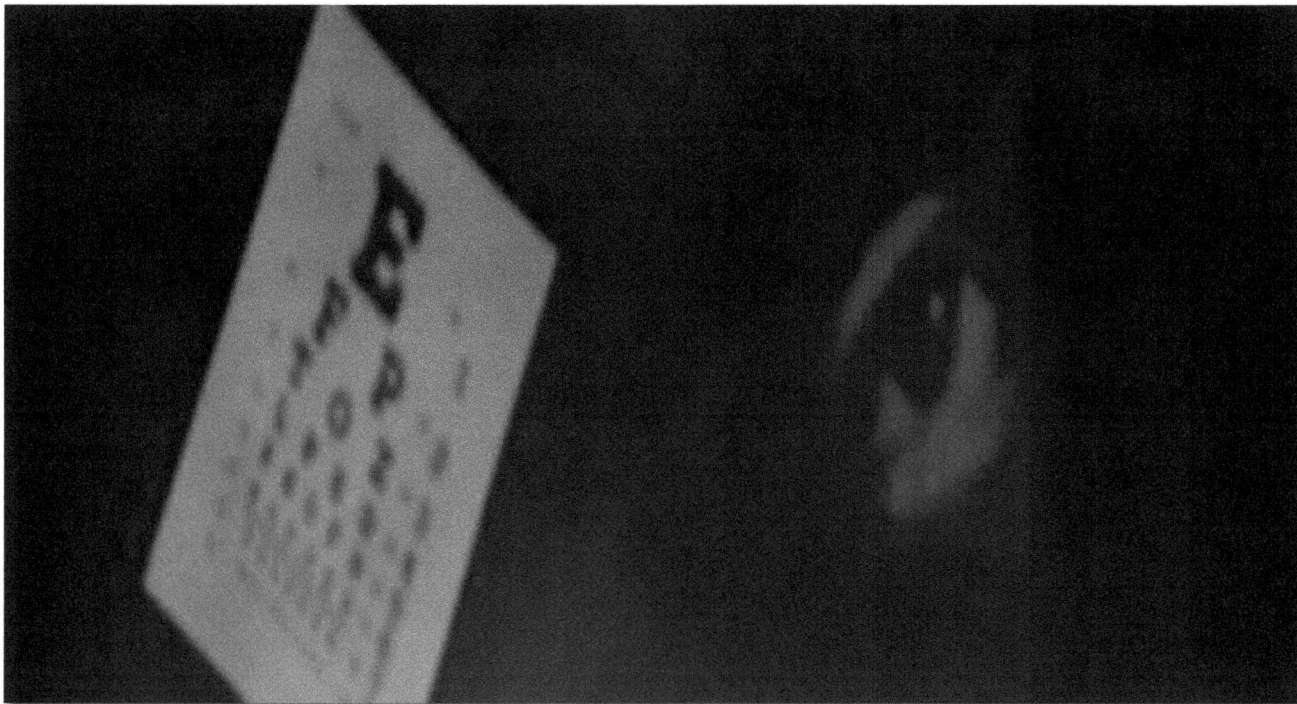

EYE TEST (2024)

John Hilliard's Eye Test (2024) masterfully explores the interplay between vision and perception through a striking composition. The photograph juxtaposes a close-up depiction of a human eye with a classic Snellen eye chart, symbolizing the act of seeing and its scientific measurement. Set against a dark, minimalist background, the dramatic lighting emphasizes the stark contrast between the eye's nuanced reflection and the chart's bold precision. Hilliard's work invites contemplation on the nature of observation, optics, and the subjectivity of sight, while the moody atmosphere elevates the image to a thought-provoking study of human perception and its inherent complexities.

meticulous and innovative. He explained, "With analogue photography, the equipment and materials fall within industry-defined parameters, yet the potential for producing radically different versions of the 'same' image is enormous. My experimentation is concerned with testing those combinations, especially where their pairing might be deemed unlikely or undesirable."

> John Hilliard's pioneering work masterfully transforms technical flaws into profound artistic statements, redefining photography's role in contemporary art.

The intentional use of "errors" like blur and overexposure is central to Hilliard's practice. He described his work as "a catalogue of errors," a phrase that balances humor with seriousness. "Blurred, unfocused, or overexposed images may be seen as mistakes," he said, "but these qualities are specific to photography. They are to be celebrated, not denied."

Balancing technical precision with emotional depth is a hallmark of Hilliard's work.

He shared, "My first step is often an idea, transcribed into notes or sketches. Techniques are either embedded in the original idea or selected afterward. Any emotional content emerges as a final part of the process, often surprising me as much as the viewer."

One of Hilliard's most profound observations is about photography's role in capturing the transient nature of the world. He described photography as a "fugitive medium" that parallels the impermanence of life. "Photography itself is always decaying, always transient," he said. "Yet, it remains a useful tool for arresting and affirming events at a particular time and place."

However, Hilliard acknowledged the challenges posed by the digital age. "In a 'post-truth' environment facilitated by digital technology, the photograph's credibility as evidence is undermined," he cautioned. "We need to be doubly alert to the wilful dismantling of photographic veracity."

John Hilliard's work transcends the visual, engaging viewers in a dialogue about truth, representation, and the fleeting nature of reality. His innovative approach and philosophical depth continue to inspire artists and audiences alike, cementing his legacy as a true pioneer in the art of photography.

Exploring Boundaries, Connections, And Transformation In Contemporary Art

Jean Alexander Frater Redefines Painting Through Sculpture And Material Experimentation

Jean Alexander Frater deconstructs painting's core materials, blending sculpture, abstraction, and craft to create transformative works that challenge conventions and explore embodiment, labor, and material limits.

"
"Paradoxically, I find that these limitations open up new possibilities."

JEAN ALEXANDER FRATER

Mixed Media

Jean Alexander Frater is an artist whose practice boldly reimagines the traditions of painting, sculpture, and craft. Her work transcends conventional categorizations, occupying a space where materials, histories, and artistic forms converge. Guided by a deep intellectual curiosity and a background in philosophy, Frater transforms paint, canvas, and the rectilinear frame into vehicles for experimentation, challenging viewers to reconsider what they know about art. This exploration of her creative process and philosophy is adapted from an insightful interview originally published in *WOWwART* magazine.

Frater's art is a testament to the power of limitation and possibility. Working primarily with paint, canvas, and the rectilinear frame—materials she defines as the core of painting—she deconstructs and reinterprets their traditional roles. "Paradoxically, I find that these limitations open up new possibili-

ties," Frater explains. This approach is exemplified in her piece *Navy Bead*, where the pictorial image within a rectangular frame is reimagined as a sculptural form. The painting's image exists simultaneously as a physical object—a pod-like, hanging structure composed of coiled canvas and frame. This technique, influenced by her years of working with ceramics, highlights her fascination with material limits and their potential for transformation.

Her work often exists in the liminal space between categories: painting and sculpture, traditional craft and contemporary abstraction, form and function. "I see all of my work as existing between categories," she notes. This exploration is driven by a desire to discover what something can become through the journey of material and language. For instance, her piece *Escaping the Beauty Instrument* embodies this fluidity, evolving from a sketch to a color-field painting and finally into a form that evokes a pitcher, a harp, and a vessel. The title reflects her exploration of the gaze, beauty, and the interplay between abstraction and form.

Frater's background in philosophy deeply informs her artistic practice. Her undergraduate studies opened new ways of thinking about the relationship between body, labor, gender, and materiality. After a decade-long focus on ceramics, she pursued graduate studies, where painting became the primary medium through which she could stage these concerns. "Ultimately, my experiments are about breaking free from fixed definitions—allowing the traditional

Jean Alexander Frater is an extraordinary artist who redefines art, showcasing innovation and a profound philosophical approach.

'rules' of painting to be bent, shifted, and at times, completely reimagined," she says. This philosophy manifests in her work through a collapsing of materiality, structure, and context, creating art that is both painting and something entirely new.

Beyond her studio practice, Frater is deeply engaged in fostering artistic community. Her experience as a BOLT resident with the Chicago Artists Coalition was transformative. Over the course of a year, she shared a space with eleven other artists from diverse disciplines, participating in solo exhibitions, critique sessions, and studio visits with art

professionals. This environment nurtured both her creative work and her commitment to community building. "This rigorous environment fostered both creative work and community building," she reflects. It inspired her to establish *Material*, a nonprofit artist-run space dedicated to collaboration and artistic exploration.

Frater's international exhibitions and contributions to the arts community highlight her influence as both an artist and a thought leader. Her work is not only a dialogue with materials and forms but also an invitation to engage with art as a site of connection and transformation.

Jean Alexander Frater's art challenges us to see the familiar in new ways, to embrace the tension between limitation and possibility, and to celebrate the beauty of process and change. As she continues to push the boundaries of painting, her work remains a poignant reminder of art's power to connect, inspire, and transform.

Jean Alexander Frater's Escaping the Beauty Instrument (2024) is a masterful exploration of abstraction and materiality. Measuring 60 x 56 inches, this bold work merges painting and sculpture, blurring traditional boundaries. Frater's layered and deconstructed approach transforms canvas and paint, offering a textured, tactile composition with intertwining organic forms. The piece evokes movement and depth, with every element engaging in a dialogue of balance and transformation. This artwork reflects Frater's dedication to pushing the limits of visual language, turning the act of painting into a multidimensional, philosophical exploration of form and meaning.

PHOTO: *A Festive Celebration of German Culture: Traditional Attire, Delicious Food, and Smiles at the Bar*

The Munich Cricket Club
Where Germany Meets London in Spectacular Style!

The Munich Cricket Club in Victoria offers an immersive Bavarian experience in London, with authentic décor and a warm welcome. The menu blends German and British cuisines, complemented by a variety of drinks. While desserts could improve, the lively atmosphere and themed events make it a must-visit destination for a taste of Oktoberfest year-round.

The Munich Cricket Club in London offers an authentic Bavarian experience with delicious food, lively atmosphere, and warm hospitality. Prost!

BY
LESLEY
MCHARG

When you step into The Munich Cricket Club, you're not just entering a restaurant; you're embarking on a lively, unforgettable journey into the heart of Bavaria. With three vibrant branches spread across London – Tower Hill, Victoria, and Canary Wharf – our recent visit to the Victoria location left us buzzing with excitement.

From the moment you ascend the stairs to the entrance, where an impressive display of German steins piques your curiosity, you know you're in for something special. Descending into the restaurant itself, the first thing that strikes you is the incredible sense of light and space, an unexpected surprise for a basement venue. With its high ceilings and unique lighting, The Munich Cricket Club successfully blends coziness with an open, inviting ambiance.

The interior design is a masterpiece of authenticity, transporting you straight to a traditional German beer hall. Wooden benches, long communal tables, checkered tablecloths, beer barrels, and charming wall displays adorned with beer labels and lederhosen create an atmosphere that is unmistakably Bavarian. It's as if Munich has been magically transported to the heart of London.

A highlight of our visit was the warm and friendly welcome we received from Florian, the General Manager, and his staff, all dressed in traditional German/Bavarian costumes. Their goal is clear: to recreate the spirit of Germany's Oktoberfest year-round while infusing it with the best of British hospitality. And thus, The Munich Cricket Club was born.

The menu is a tantalizing fusion of German and British delights. There's a wide selection of drinks, including flavored schnapps and a beer taster board for the beer enthusiasts among us. The cocktails, with their contemporary German twist, are a must-try. We couldn't get enough of the Apple Strudel Martini and the cheekily named German Pornstar. The food is a hearty affair with generous portions, featuring classics like goulash, noodles, schnitzel, currywurst, and sauerkraut. It's a culinary journey that transports your taste buds straight to Germany, right in the heart of bustling London.

While most dishes delighted our palates, we couldn't help but feel that the desserts, especially the apple strudel and German cheesecake, had room for improvement.

The Munich Cricket Club is not just a restaurant; it's an experience. It's the perfect spot for weekend brunches, post-work happy hour drinks, hen dos, stag dos, and private parties with two dedicated function areas. And the exciting news is that three branches are already lighting up London, with a fourth on the horizon.

The only disappointment of our visit? Missing out on the Thursday night extravaganza featuring live music, Oompah Bands, and the joy of dancing on the tables. Next time, we won't make that mistake. The Munich Cricket Club beckons with its promise of unbridled fun, delicious fare, and an atmosphere that transports you to the heart of Bavaria. Prost!

> " The Munich Cricket Club in London masterfully brings Bavarian charm with authentic décor, hearty cuisine, and lively events, creating unforgettable experiences. "

Nilay Aydin Brings Middle Eastern Magic To 215 Hackney, Creating A Cosy Oasis Of Culinary Excellence In Stoke Newington

BY
BEN. F. ONCU

"

215 Hackney by Nilay Aydin offers Middle Eastern-inspired cuisine with creative flair, intimate ambiance, and extraordinary dishes like Shakshuka, Baklava French Toast, and Morning Palestine breakfast platter in Stoke Newington.

Mehmet and Nilay Aydin, a dynamic young couple and enterprising restaurateurs, have recently brought to life 215 Hackney—a Middle Eastern-inspired café that's much more than just a place to eat. Opened a few months ago, this cosy spot in Stoke Newington has quickly become a favourite among locals and visitors alike. Mrs Aydin, the head chef and culinary visionary, takes charge of the kitchen, crafting every dish with the warmth and authenticity of homemade food. Their dedication to quality and passion for hospitality has turned this intimate café into a hub of community and gastronomic artistry.

Before the food even arrives, 215 Hackney captivates you with its stunning interior design. The space is a harmonious blend of modern minimalism and vintage charm, accented by subtle Middle Eastern touches that make the ambience unique. From intricately patterned décor to thoughtfully curated art pieces, every detail of the café exudes warmth and sophistication. The layout strikes a balance between spaciousness and intimacy, with open seating complemented by secluded corners for a quieter experience.

> # 215 Hackney excels as a w elcoming hub, combining inventive Middle Eastern dishes, thoughtful ambiance, and outstanding hospitality to create unforgettable dining experiences.

Whether bathed in natural light during the day or softly illuminated in the evenings, the lighting creates a welcoming and cosy atmosphere. The combination of cleanliness, comfort, and thoughtful design ensures that dining here is not just enjoyable but memorable.

215 Hackney excels as a welcoming hub, combining inventive Middle Eastern dishes, thoughtful ambiance, and outstanding hospitality to create unforgettable dining experiences.

Shakshuka

The Shakshuka at 215 Hackney is a standout dish that bridges the gap between comfort food and culinary sophistication. Here, the familiar framework of eggs poached in a rich tomato and pepper sauce is taken to new heights. The eggs are cooked to perfection, their golden yolks adding a luscious richness to the velvety and robust sauce alive with the freshness of ripe tomatoes, aromatic peppers, and fragrant herbs.

The dish is elevated further by its thoughtful accompaniments: a toasted za'atar pitta bread sprinkled generously with spices, and a cooling dollop of lima yoghurt that provides a refreshing tang and cuts through the richness beautifully. Every bite is a harmonious interplay of creamy, chunky, and zesty textures, making the Shakshuka a crowd favourite that's as satisfying as it is flavour-forward.

Morning Palestine

The Morning Palestine breakfast platter is a culinary masterpiece that showcases the depth and richness of Middle Eastern tradition. At its centre is the Jerusalem bagel, a sesame-crusted triumph that balances crispness with a soft, pillowy interior. Paired with homemade tahini butter and a drizzle of honey, it offers a delicious combination of nutty sweetness.

Golden fried eggs are sprinkled with sumac and black sesame seeds, creating vibrant, tangy accents to their richness. Persian olives, creamy organic feta, and smoky grilled halloumi impart layers of briny and savoury flavours, while the muhammara and hummus dips add bold, spiced undertones that tie the dish together. Fresh, hearty, and indulgent, this platter exemplifies the ethos of 215 Hackney: thoughtful dishes that celebrate tradition with a touch of modern flair.

Jerusalem Platter

The Jerusalem platter is a showstopper, especially for those seeking either traditional or plant-based options. Anchored by warm, fluffy homemade pitta, the dish features bold, luxurious dips such as feta hummus and smoky babaganoush. Boiled eggs and turmeric yoghurt add a comforting richness, while the vegan option with turmeric-scrambled tofu is equally impressive, offering flavour and texture without compromise.

The walnut dak dak salad introduces crunch and freshness to the platter, complemented by the briny juiciness of Nocellara olives. Together, these elements create a balanced and deeply satisfying meal that celebrates the versatility of Middle Eastern cuisine. The Jerusalem platter is a testament to Hackney's ability to seamlessly blend tradition and creativity into one harmonious dish.

Beyond its exceptional food, 215 Hackney radiates heart and soul thanks to Mehmet and Nilay's passion for hospitality. The café feels less like a commercial space and more like an extension of their home—warm, inviting, and infused with creativity. Whether you're coming for a leisurely brunch or a special celebration, the duo's attention to detail ensures every visit feels unique and welcoming.

Dining at 215 Hackney is an experience that transcends eating; it's a journey through flavours, traditions, and craftsmanship. From the bold Shakshuka to the

playful Baklava French Toast, each dish is a testament to Mrs Aydin's skill and ingenuity. This café is a shining example of why Stoke Newington has become a foodie haven. Whether you're here for comfort food or to explore culinary artistry, 215 Hackney delivers on every front. Highly recommended for anyone looking to savour Middle Eastern-inspired cuisine in a cosy and stylish setting.

> *The Morning Palestine breakfast platter is a culinary masterpiece that showcases the depth and richness of Middle Eastern tradition.*

A Culinary Voyage to South West Coastal India, Infused with Michelin-Star Magic

BY
KIRSTY
ROWE

" Embarking on a culinary odyssey at Quilon is akin to savouring the symphony of South West Coastal India on a plate – where Michelin-star excellence harmonizes with vibrant flavours, creating an unforgettable gastronomic masterpiece.

Located in the heart of London, just a stone's throw away from Buckingham Palace, Quilon Restaurant offers a gastronomic experience that's a harmonious blend of Michelin-star excellence and the vibrant flavours of South West Coastal Indian cuisine. During a recent weekend brunch outing, I had the pleasure of immersing myself in their celebrated Onam Brunch menu – an offering that beautifully captured the essence of this culinary tradition.

From the moment I walked in, Quilon's elegant ambience and attentive service set the stage for a memorable dining experience. The Onam Brunch, available every Saturday and Sunday, was an exploration of vegetarian and non-vegetarian delights from the region, each dish meticulously curated by the talented team led by Chef Sriram Aylur.

Sriram's lifelong passion for food began in his father's kitchen. Inspired by his father's joyful approach to cooking, he pursued culinary education, eventually joining Taj Hotels. After honing his skills, he opened the renowned Karavali Restaurant. He later established Quilon in London, blending traditional and innovative South-west Indian cuisine. Quilon garnered numerous awards, including a Michelin Star, reflecting Sriram's progressive culinary vision and dedication to his craft.

The staff, as kind as they were knowledgeable, played an integral role in enhancing the entire experience. Each dish was presented with a fascinating introduction, delving into its origin and distinct flavours. This insight added an extra layer of enjoyment, allowing a deeper connection with the cuisine.

The Onam Brunch, both Vegetarian and Non-Vegetarian, bore the hallmark of Chef Sriram Aylur's culinary finesse. I delved into the Vegetarian Onam Brunch, a symphony of tastes that delighted the senses. The culinary adventure commenced with a sweet potato s-a-a-a-t, a harmonious blend of textures and flavours that left a delightful crunch. The water kosambri in a watermelon cup followed, a palate-cleansing marvel that was both fresh and invigorating.

The journey began with an assortment of traditional Indian snacks that included coin papadam, banana chips, jackfruit chips, sarkara varatti, chutneys, and pickles. This delightful array of crunchy bites provided a glimpse into the diverse textures and flavours that awaited.

The appetizers that followed were a testament to the restaurant's dedication to authenticity and innovation. The stuffed tapioca chop with its mint sauce was a surprising fusion of textures, while the banana flower vada paired with curry leaf chutney provided a tantalizing play of flavours. The mini masala dosa, served with sambhar, was a mini marvel of crispiness and spiciness.

The main courses were a true celebration of Kerala's culinary heritage. The kada chakka thiyal, a traditional Keralan breadfruit curry, showcased aromatic spices that danced on the palate. Olan, a coconut milk-based stew with black-eyed beans and ash gourd, offered a subtle balance of richness and lightness. Avial, a medley of South Indian vegetables seasoned with coconut, delivered a symphony of tastes and textures.

The erissery, pumpkin cooked with coconut and spices, was a comforting dish with a harmonious blend of flavors. Vellarikka pachadi, a Kerala cucumber raita, provided a cooling contrast. The

beans and carrot thoran, with its mild spices and crunchy vegetables, was a perfect accompaniment to the flavourful coconut red rice and fluffy steamed rice.

The star of the show was undoubtedly the malabar paratha – a flaky, multi-layered bread that served as the perfect vessel for savouring the diverse curries. The meal concluded on a sweet note with ada pradaman, pal payasam, and pazam pori – each dessert showcasing the artistry of traditional Indian sweets.

Quilon's Onam Brunch is an exploration of flavours that transport you to the sun-soaked shores of South West Coastal India. While the dining experience is undoubtedly exceptional, the complexity and authenticity of the dishes might be better appreciated by

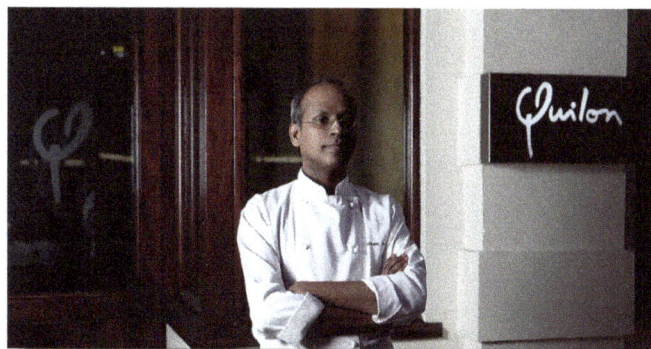

those familiar with Indian cuisine. The brunch presents an excellent opportunity to delve into the nuances of Keralan food, and with its stunning location and culinary prowess, Quilon is a must-visit destination for those seeking a gourmet adventure in London.

Quilon Restaurant is more than just a dining establishment; it's a sensory journey through the rich tapestry of South West Coastal Indian cuisine. From the serene ambiance to the knowledgeable staff, and most importantly, the tantalizing dishes crafted by Chef Sriram Aylur, every aspect converges to create an unforgettable experience. Whether you're a connoisseur of Indian cuisine or a curious epicurean, Quilon promises a culinary odyssey that's worth savouring. The brunch presents an excellent opportunity to delve into the nuances of Keralan food, and with its stunning location and culinary prowess, Quilon is a must-visit destination for those seeking a gourmet adventure in London.

> ## Quilon Restaurant offers a Michelin-starred South West Indian culinary journey near Buckingham Palace, with exceptional service and exquisite dishes.

Quilon, nestled in Buckingham Gate, once hosted guests of Buckingham Palace and still exudes the elegance of those days with its refined interior and serene atmosphere. Executive chef Sriram Aylur brings to life the essence of modern southern Indian coastal cuisine, using the freshest ingredients to blend traditional home-cooking with contemporary dishes.

A Journey Through Flavour and Style With Afrikana Holloway

BY
BEN F. ONCU

"Afrikana Holloway delivers a vibrant experience with African inspired cuisine, stunning interior design, exceptional service, and great value for money, making it a must-visit restaurant in London.

Afrikana Holloway delivers a vibrant experience with African-inspired cuisine, stunning interior design, exceptional service, and great value for money, making it a must-visit restaurant in London.

Last year, I first discovered Afrikana when I saw its vibrant facade in various cities. It immediately caught my attention. Later, as I came across its branchei in Holloway, curiosity sparked even further. Yet, despite my intrigue, it took me quite a while to finally pay them a visit. From its exterior, Afrikana appeared to be an elegant restaurant with a lively cultural vibe. It made me wonder about its menu offerings—would it showcase traditional African cuisine, or perhaps modern interpretations of flavours from the continent? Was this a celebration of South African dishes, Nigerian feasts, Kenyan classics, or even Senegalese delights? As someone unfamiliar with African culinary heritage back then, the notion of stepping into Afrikana intrigued me deeply.

All these speculations finally came to life when I visited Afrikana Holloway. To say my expectations were exceeded would be an understatement—the food, the atmosphere, and the overall experience were far beyond what I'd imagined. Looking back, I can't believe how much I'd deprived myself by delaying

this visit. One thing I can confidently say after being there: if you're a fan of Nando's, you'll love Afrikana even more. It brings new dimensions to dishes you might find familiar, offering flavours that are richer, deeper, and

even more satisfying. And if hearty meat platters or grilled steak are your go-to, Afrikana should be high on your must-visit list.

Walking into Afrikana Holloway, I was struck by its ambiance. The space feels lively

Afrikana Holloway blends vibrant Afrocentric decor with contemporary elegance, creating a warm and inviting atmosphere for an unforgettable dining experience.

Elevate your dining experience at The Madera Restaurant, where chic meets enchanting treehouse vibes high above London's Langham Place.

yet polished, with a stylish blend of contemporary decor and cultural expression. The walls are adorned with bold and colourful artwork, showcasing striking depictions of African traditions and heritage. From vibrant tribal patterns to portraits interwoven with natural themes, every piece speaks to the roots of the continent while energising the dining area. The furniture complements the aesthetic perfectly—sleek, modern touches like deep-green leather booths and earthy wooden tables are paired with pops of colour from cushioned benches. The use of textures such as woven lighting fixtures and rattan-backed chairs creates an intriguing interplay that feels warm and inviting. Faux greenery, including indoor trees and lush planters, adds to the atmosphere, lending the restaurant a refreshing and tranquil vibe.

Even the lighting deserves mention for its thoughtful design. By day, the large windows flood the space with natural sunlight, making it feel airy. By evening, the warm glow of pendant lamps softens the tone and transforms the room into something cosier. Combined with illuminated artwork on the walls, there's always an uplifting and engaging feel to Afrikana Holloway.

When it came to the food, the standout dish—and one I won't forget—is Afrikana's We Meat Again platter. Sharing this feast with a colleague was an unforgettable experience. It's hard to do justice to just how generous and varied this dish is. The platter brings together a delicious assortment of perfectly cooked meats: two tender lamb chops, three grilled chicken wings coated in a smoky glaze, a whole marinated chicken bursting with rich flavours, two hearty 4oz steaks

expertly seasoned and grilled, and the house special prawns—a true highlight, fresh, bold, and spiced impeccably. On the side, we enjoyed offerings that uniquely complemented the meat selection: fries, jollof rice (a famous West African dish packed with tomato and spice flavours), rice 'n peas, and coleslaw. We also added plantain to the mix—a fried banana with a texture and taste reminiscent of soft, buttery potatoes. Every bite was a harmony of freshness, bold seasoning, and complementary textures.

Even beyond taste, the presentation of We Meat Again was noteworthy. Served on a large wooden board, the meats were placed thoughtfully, showcasing their caramelised glazes and succulent textures. The sides were arranged elegantly, creating a feast that appealed not just to the palate but also to the eyes. As for the portion size, it was more than generous—ideal for sharing among two or even three diners.

What impressed me the most was how well each component was cooked to perfection. The lamb chops were juicy with just the right smokiness. The chicken wings balanced spice and sweetness beautifully while the whole chicken remained tender and flavourful. The steaks were hearty and rich, while the prawns delivered cutting-edge freshness and depth of seasoning. Even the sides enhanced the dish further—whether it was the jollof rice bursting with spice or the creamy and refreshing coleslaw that balanced the meal's richness.

The overall experience at Afrikana Hollo-

way was elevated further by its service and cleanliness. The staff were welcoming, professional, and knowledgeable about the menu, offering clear recommendations and answering our queries with ease. Waiting times were minimal, reflecting a well-coordinated kitchen and attentive floor staff. The restaurant's cleanliness couldn't go unnoticed; everything from table settings to flooring sparkled, which added comfort to the dining experience.

Afrikana Holloway offers exceptional value for money. Despite the premium quality of the food and level of care put into the service, the pricing remains reasonable. For a dish as diverse, abundant, and flavourful as We Meat Again, the value truly feels unmatched. From the moment you step in, the restaurant delivers more than just a meal—it provides an experience rooted in rich flavours, vibrant cultural decoration, and welcoming service.

If you've ever enjoyed Nando's, Afrikana is likely to surpass your expectations. It takes familiar flavours and elevates them, providing a broader menu and more diverse, exciting choices for meat lovers and adventurous diners. Whether you're exploring African cuisine for the first time or celebrating a special occasion, Afrikana Holloway offers an unforgettable experience. Don't wait as long as I did to visit—it's a gem waiting to impress you, and once you've been, you'll wonder why you hadn't discovered it sooner.

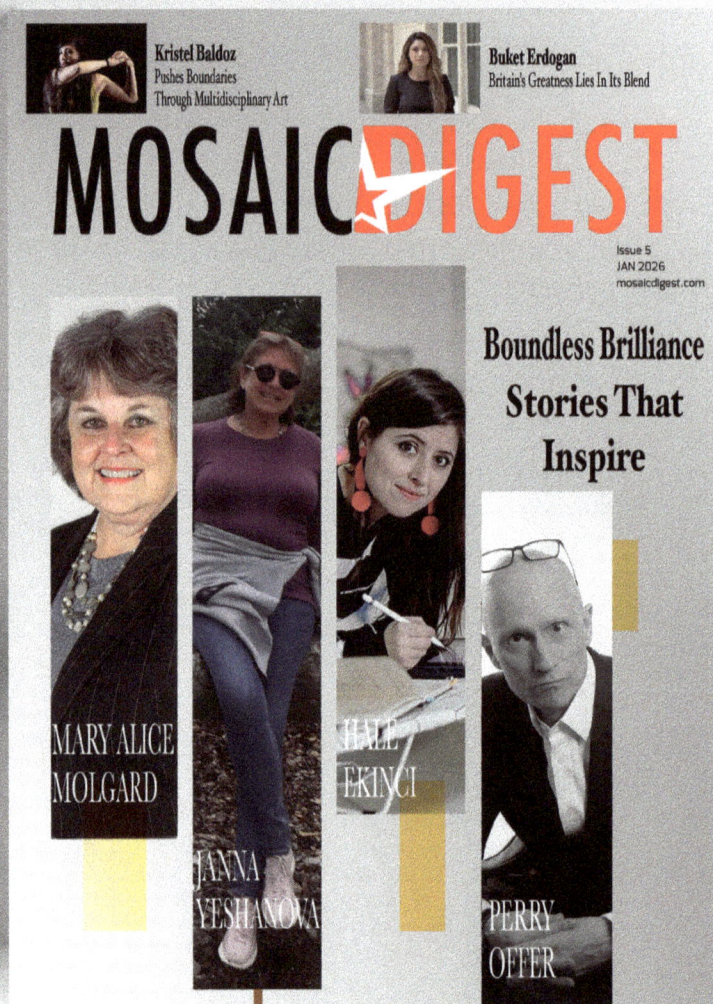

Kristel Baldoz
Pushes Boundaries
Through Multidisciplinary Art

Buket Erdogan
Britain's Greatness Lies In Its Blend

MOSAIC DIGEST

Issue 5
JAN 2026
mosaicdigest.com

Boundless Brilliance
Stories That
Inspire

MARY ALICE MOLGARD

JANNA YESHANOVA

HALE EKINCI

PERRY OFFER

Available in
PRINT

Americas to Australia Europe to Africa Mosaic Digest is available over 190 countries and thousands of retaiers, platforms including Amazon, Barnes & Noble, Walmart, Waterstone's .....

ELECTRONIC

It is an electronic (flip book) format and interactive. Accessable from electronic devices like pc, smart phone, notepads..

ONLINE

All interviews, we conduct make them accessable online for free.

SOCIAL MEDIA

We are on Facebook, Instagram and X. Please follow us on social media @mosaicdigest

contact us today for an interview opportunity at
editor@mosaicdigest.com

And so much more ...

Key Partnerships and Future Initiatives
Expanding the Boundaries of Art and Media

*Being featured in Mosaic Digest means gaining visibility
not just in print edition, but across the entire media
spectrum in the US, UK, Europe and beyond*

Key Media Partnerships:

- Associated Press (reaching 50%+ of global population)
- Benzinga (5M monthly visitors)
- Nexstar (68% U.S. TV household penetration)
- Major search engines: Google News, Google, Yahoo, Bing, Ask
- EIN Press Wire coverage
- NewYox Media magazines coverage (Mosaic Digest, Reader's House, CEO Vision, Beauty Prime...)

Broadcast & Digital Coverage:

- Major U.S. network affiliates
- 150+ million monthly radio website users
- 500+ UK media outlets
- Minimum 5 to 20 media placements per country (Albania to Zambia)
- Enhanced SEO positioning with quality backlinks from each media
- Optimized presence on e-commerce platforms)

Distribution Highlights:

- Available through major retailers including Amazon, Barnes & Noble, Walmart, Blackwells and Waterstones
- Available through local retailers Alaska to Wisconsin in the United States.
- Available in print LIFETIME
- Featured across 3000+ media platforms in the US, UK, Europe and beyond

contact us today for an interview opportunity at
editor@mosaicdigest.com